Successful
TOURISM
MARKETING

A Practical Handbook

SUSAN BRIGGS

KOGAN
PAGE

**To Mary, Malcolm, Paula and Elias for all
their love and support**

First published in 1997

Kogan Page Limited
120 Pentonville Road
London N1 9JN

British Library Cataloguing in Publication Data

A CIP record for this book is available from the British Library.

ISBN 0 7494 2123 1

Typeset by Kogan Page Ltd
Printed and bound in Great Britain by Biddles Ltd, Guildford and Kings Lynn

CONTENTS

Section Four: Case studies and examples of good marketing   173

ACKNOWLEDGEMENTS

The author wishes to thank the following for their help and support in the writing of this book:

Catriona Campbell

Paul Hopper and Rebecca Milton at the London Tourist Board

Helen Carpenter at Discover Islington

Dorothy Williams, Dean Gorddard and Chris Thorne at Wiltshire County Council

Neena Sohal at Pitshanger Manor Museum

David Miles and Ann Wilson at Historic Royal Palaces Agency

Press Office at the British Tourist Authority

INTRODUCTION

Early into the next century travel and tourism will be the world's largest industry. Tourism is worth around £37 billion to the UK economy and the UK accounts for 5 per cent of world tourism receipts. Tourism employs some 1.7 million people in the UK but it is a highly fragmented industry with around 200,000 businesses competing to attract domestic and overseas visitors. With improved marketing most tourism businesses could claim a bigger share of this lucrative industry.

This book will be of benefit to anyone seeking to promote a tourism 'product' or service, whether it is a destination, visitor attraction, hotel or tour operation. It aims to offer practical information and advice directly related to the tourism industry, which can be easily applied.

Rather than concentrate solely on marketing principles, the first section looks at the tourism industry, considering some of the markets for tourism products, so you can develop a picture of some of the markets you may wish to target. The second section will take you through each aspect of a marketing plan and the third offers practical advice about the use of promotional 'tools'. The final section describes real examples of good practice and successful marketing activities.

1

THE TOURISM INDUSTRY

There have been many attempts to define tourism. The Tourism Society uses one of the most enduring definitions, put forward by Burkitt and Medley in *Tourism, Past, Present & Future* (published by Heinemann in 1974) who define it as: 'the temporary short term movement of people to destinations outside places where they normally live and work, and their activities during their stay at these destinations'.

It is easy to refer glibly to 'tourists' as if they were an anonymous mass of people, but of course there are many different types of tourist. Each group, or segment, has different needs and motivations.

Tourists may be international visitors from another country or a family who have just travelled a couple of hours to see their relatives and go out together. The latter are often referred to as VFR – visit(or)s to friends and relatives. They do not always book accommodation but are often a good market for attractions. It is when Auntie Nellie and the Gang come to stay that many families visit attractions, travelling in a sizeable group, staying longer and spending more than they usually would at attractions.

'Tourists' are usually taken to be people who are temporarily staying at least one night in an area. The word 'visitors' is a more umbrella term, meaning tourists, excursionists and locals on a day out. 'Tourist' is sometimes used pejoratively. For this reason, and because it is a generic term, ' visitor' is used more widely.

Before beginning to plan or undertake any marketing activities it is important to be clear about target markets, which will vary for every tourism business. This section gives an overview of some of the different markets within the tourism industry. Understanding the various components of the travel trade will make it easier to target.

THE TRAVEL TRADE

The travel trade is a complex mixture of voluntary and commercial sector organisations and usually acts as an intermediary between the public and tourism products. Many visitors travel independently so promotions should not be targeted solely at the travel trade. Nonetheless there are several important advantages to working with the travel trade:

▒ It can be difficult to directly influence independent visitors, so working with the travel trade is often an easier way of developing visitor and guest numbers.

▒ It is a very cost-effective marketing method – the travel trade has multiple purchasing power so once you have identified one key decision maker they can bring numerous visitors, either as individuals or in groups.

▒ The travel trade usually pre-book visits so they can form a good core business, and give you an opportunity to plan staffing, etc. Because they pre-book, groups and the travel trade are sometimes more reliable visitors than individuals. For example garden attractions suffer from lower visitor numbers in bad weather but pre-booked groups still visit.

▒ The travel trade can be persuaded to feature 'off-peak' visits, when there are fewer other visitors.

▒ Although they usually demand discounts or commissions, groups will sometimes pay extra for additional services such as behind-the-scenes tours and special talks.

The travel trade comprises:

▨ travel agents;

▨ tour operators;

▨ handling agents, incoming tour operators and ground handlers;

▨ coach operators;

▨ group travel organisers;

▨ short break operators;

▨ incentive houses;

▨ corporate hospitality organisers and conference organisers.

Carriers such as airlines and ferries could also be included in this category, particularly when they offer their own programmes comprising accommodation and sightseeing packages.

Travel agents

Travel agents sell holidays to the public, acting as retail distributors for tour operators and carriers. They make their living through commission payments and overrides. As the name implies, business travel agents specialise in flight and accommodation bookings for business travellers. Reservation and booking agents are similar to travel agents but usually specialise in one aspect such as accommodation bookings.

Although they are a part of the travel trade, there is little point in targeting travel agents directly, as most of them simply make bookings from tour operators' brochures.

Tour operators

Tour operators package the individual components of a holiday or tour, negotiating inclusive fares for travel, accommodation, transfers, sightseeing, etc. Many sell their products through brochures racked in travel agencies. Some are direct-sell operations, using direct mail and selling 'off the page' in newspapers and magazines.

Handling agents, incoming tour operators and ground handlers

These three categories are often grouped together even though they are slightly different. The work of all of them begins and ends when clients from overseas (who will often have made their bookings through an overseas tour operator) step on to and leave British soil. All other services such as travel to the UK are handled from overseas.

Handling agents and ground handlers react according to their clients' demand, organising transfers from points of entry to hotels, making hotel bookings and arranging sightseeing excursions. Incoming tour operators may have their own programme and brochure from which clients may buy. Many offer tailor made services, so are equally reactive and work on a more *ad hoc* basis. However, many handling agents and ground handlers call themselves incoming tour operators so the distinction is sometimes only academic.

In some cases overseas clients know exactly what they want to book, especially if they are arranging standard tours such as a four-day London programme for first time visitors to London. Sometimes incoming tour operators have the opportunity to be more creative, particularly if researching and booking special interest tours.

I was once asked to arrange a tour of England on behalf of a German police society. Their leader requested a special 'gag' for the last day – could I possibly encourage the British police to stop the coach and arrest everyone for a couple of hours!

Incoming tour operators work through a long distribution chain. For example, a French person may buy a package from a travel agent, who will book the package with a tour operator, who may have bought it from a package travel wholesaler, who could have contracted the hotels through a ground handler based in London. This means that they need you to react very quickly (within 24 hours) to requests for information, etc and bear in mind that prices may be marked up several times before they reach the end-user or consumer.

The British Incoming Tour Operators' Association lists around 125 full members in its *Handbook and Membership List*, which costs around £30 from:

BITOA
120 Wilton Street
London
SW1
Telephone 0171 931 0601.

Coach operators

These range from huge operators such as Wallace Arnold who publish their own brochure of coaching holidays, to small driver-owner or family-run companies whose business is mainly private hire contracts from group organisers and local societies.

Coach operators used to be considered the poor relations of the travel trade, generating low value visits from large groups of aged people dawdling crocodile fashion to the tea shop. Group sizes seem to have decreased in recent years to around 30 people, with increasingly affluent passengers.

Many coach tours are booked by active senior citizens who are living longer and who have a higher disposable income, so they are a good market. Coach tours and holidays are also booked by people looking for a second or third annual holiday.

It is sometimes worth approaching the larger coach operators to persuade them to include your product in their programme. Some of the smaller coach operators are asked to suggest places to visit by group organisers but in the majority of cases they come to coach operators with a fixed idea about where they want to go.

Short break operators

Short break operators may be hotel chains who publish their own short break brochures to sell empty hotel rooms at weekends.

There are also several major operators who include accommodation of one to four nights, optional transport and sightseeing excursions. This is a growth market, albeit a competitive one, and short break operators are continually looking for new destinations and activities to package.

Incentive agents and corporate hospitality

Travel can be used as a motivator for staff or clients. Incentive agents typically look for events and itineraries which are not accessible to the general public, which makes the trip more special. Corporate hospitality works in a similar way, often using an event like a day trip to the races as a basic component, and adding on extras such as entrance to a special enclosure, gourmet lunch and souvenir programme.

Group travel organisers

A recent survey estimated there are around 6000 independent and active group travel organisers (referred to as GTOs), many of whom work on a voluntary basis.

The majority of group travel organisations surveyed were retirement and social clubs, with over 41 per cent of all organisations made up of people aged over 60. Organisations which generate group outings on a voluntary basis include:

▒ women's groups such as Women's Institutes, Townswomen's Guilds and Fellowship Clubs;

▒ social clubs such as staff social clubs or 'day-out' clubs;

▒ retirement associations such as Probus and company retirement clubs;

▒ special interest groups such as arts clubs and universities of the third age.

Lists of these organisations can be obtained from list brokers, or they can be targeted through publications such as *Group Travel*

Organiser magazine. Many organisations are listed in the *Directory of British Associations*, but these tend to be head offices, rather than local branches. Libraries sometimes keep lists of local organisations.

NEEDS OF THE TRAVEL TRADE

You will get more business from the travel trade if you can understand and satisfy their needs. They will expect you to provide the following:

Information and publicity material

Publicity material should be clearly suitable for the travel trade. Include this information where relevant:

- Basic descriptions of your facilities – what makes you different or better than your competitors?
- Advance notice – preferably 6–12 months, and details of any events or special offers.
- Opening times and suggested duration of visits (for attractions and destinations). Information about the best time to visit is also welcomed.
- Location, preferably with a map showing coach drop-off points and coach parks.
- Details of group rates, commission structure and any special payment arrangements for the travel trade.
- Free places and special facilities for coach drivers and guides.
- Details of special arrangements for groups, such as guided tours; catering facilities or packages; discount in gift shops; out-of-hours opening; group check-in, etc.
- Contact name and telephone number for group enquiries.

Bookings and enquiries

It is important to make it easy for the travel trade to book, otherwise they will not. They need an obvious point of contact who is available during normal office hours. This should preferably be someone with a title like 'groups co-ordinator' so the travel trade feel they understand their needs.

The booking process must be straightforward and, preferably, immediate. For example, it is frustrating to telephone to make a group booking and be told that one needs a group booking form, wait for that to be sent, fill in the form, return it and then await confirmation. The more stages there are in the sales process, the less likely the travel trade are to make a definite booking.

Pricing policy and payment

Hotels are expected to offer group discounts or commission to the travel trade and most attractions also offer 10–20 per cent discount. It is general practice to offer one free place for the driver/guide or group leader if there are more than 15 people in a group.

The travel trade need flexible payment systems. Sometimes it is possible for a group leader to present a cheque or cash on arrival on behalf of the whole group. However, many members of the travel trade demand acceptance of their vouchers, either for individuals or groups, expecting you to invoice them after departure.

SCHOOLS AND EDUCATIONAL TRAVEL

Schools and educational travel organisers are not strictly part of the travel trade but they do act as booking intermediaries and generate significant business so it is worth considering them here.

Some schools and educational establishments (including English language schools) arrange outings and visits on behalf of their students, generally as part of an educational programme, so they represent an important market for visitor attractions and some destinations. Educational visits are sometimes viewed negatively because they generate low cost, young visitors who may become unruly. However, they can also generate secondary visits, bringing their families with them. Another advantage to educational visits is that they generally take place at off-peak periods.

Key points to consider about school visits are:

▓ Most school and educational visits are made to places about 60 minutes' drive-time from the educational establishment.

▓ When deciding where to visit, the following are some of the most important factors for teachers and group leaders:

  ▓ perceived educational value of the visit;
  ▓ positive experience during a previous visit;
  ▓ belief that staff at an attraction or destination understand the needs of educational groups and are good at handling them.

▓ In terms of promotional methods, word-of-mouth referrals from colleagues are considered one of the most important methods. 'Seeing is believing' so it is also productive to invite teachers to view facilities for themselves and to offer special open days.

▓ The educational nature of visits is important so information should demonstrate how visits can link to specific attainment standards or elements of the National Curriculum. It is important to provide teachers' packs and planning notes.

▓ Day visits are usually planned one to three months in advance and residential visits are planned as long as ten months in advance.

▓ Around £5 per pupil is the maximum accepted price limit – educational visits are obviously price-sensitive, although secondary spend on retail and catering can be higher than expected.

▓ The majority of school visits are made by primary and middle schools.

OVERSEAS MARKETS

Overseas visits to Britain are increasing, as is the amount of money visitors spend once they are here. Forecasts for the year 2000 predict that approximately 30 million visitors (currently around 24 million) will come to Britain and account for visitor spending of approximately £18 billion (currently around £12 billion).

Britain is now winning back the market share of world tourism which it lost during the 1980s and 1990s. Tourism is our fastest growing industry and the UK now accounts for around 5 per cent of world tourism receipts.

The British Tourist Authority (BTA) is the statutory body responsible for promoting Britain as a tourist destination worldwide. BTA works in partnership with the Scottish, English, Wales and regional tourist boards, and is a government-sponsored agency funded by the Department of National Heritage.

BTA's main responsibilities are:

▓ to promote tourism to Britain from overseas;

▓ to advise the government on tourism matters affecting Britain as a whole; and

▓ encouraging the provision and improvement of tourist amenities in Britain.

In addition to its 'head office' in London, the BTA has a network of over 40 offices overseas which handle enquiries on Britain from members of the public, travel trade and media.

External influences on international travel to Britain

Socio-economic factors, demographic trends, the travel patterns of different nationalities, and political factors all have a decisive influence on international travel to Britain.

Economic forecasts can help to determine target markets. Decisive economic factors include employment and unemployment levels, interest rates, consumer confidence and levels of disposable income.

Discretionary or disposable income (the sum left once essential living costs and other fixed costs such as mortgage repayments have been paid) is a key determinant of tourism demand.

The cost of travel is a further determinant. The worldwide trend towards deregulation of air travel should lead to reductions in air fares as competition between airlines intensifies. There is also increased competition on the Channel routes, between the ferry companies and the Channel Tunnel.

Accommodation and entertainment costs (such as shopping, eating out and entry to attractions) are equally important in determining Britain's competitiveness, as are exchange rates.

Other social factors which affect international travel trends are age, standard of living and holiday entitlement.

Factors accounting for Britain's popularity as a tourist destination

Research undertaken by the BTA has shown that visitors to Britain are attracted by several aspects:

Heritage, countryside and attractions

▓ historic cities;

▓ cathedrals and churches;

▓ castles;

▓ stately homes and their gardens;

▓ archaeological sites of major historical importance such as Stonehenge and Hadrian's Wall;

▓ industrial heritage;

▓ museums and galleries;

▓ literary heritage;

▓ tradition and pageantry;

▓ the beauty and diversity of Britain's countryside and coasts.

Entertainment and the arts

▦ the range and quality of Britain's artistic life (in London around 30 per cent of all theatre tickets are bought by overseas visitors);

▦ the visual arts – many of our galleries enjoy an excellent reputation in overseas markets;

▦ sporting events – including Wimbledon tennis, British Open golf, Five Nations rugby, the FA Cup Final and major horse races.

Accommodation

▦ Britain offers a wide spectrum of accommodation ranging from small B&Bs (bed and breakfast) to luxuriously appointed self-catering cottages and apartments.

▦ B&Bs and the opportunity they offer to stay in the home of a British family are especially popular with overseas visitors.

Shopping

▦ Britain is renowned for its shopping in terms of quality, variety and value for money.

▦ Markets remain a strong favourite with many visitors.

Visitor numbers and revenue from overseas markets

The following tables show the visitor numbers and revenues generated from overseas markets.

Visits to Britain in 1995 ('000)

Total Europe	*15990*
France	3199
Germany	2659
Irish Republic	1800
Netherlands	1431

Belgium/Luxembourg	1333
Italy	941
Spain	803
Sweden	560
Switzerland	549
Norway	439
Denmark	334
Austria	261
Israel	260
Poland	182
Greece	171
Portugal	162
Czech Republic	146
Russia	143
Finland	125
Turkey	76
Hungary	57
Yugoslavian States	46
Iceland	25
Rest of Europe	288
Total Northern America	*3884*
USA	3259
Canada	625
Total Central and South America	*358*
Brazil	107
Argentina	69
Mexico	32
Venezuela	11
Other Central and South America	68
Total Asia Pacific	*2505*
Japan	642
Australia	628
Hong Kong	175
India	170
New Zealand	135
South Korea	122
Malaysia	122

Thailand	115
Singapore	100
Rest of South East Asia	85
Pakistan	74
Taiwan	57
China	32
Other Asia Pacific	48
Total Middle East	*391*
Gulf States	216
Saudi Arabia	125
Iran	12
Other Middle East	38
Total Africa	*618*
South Africa	255
East Africa (Commonwealth)	141
Nigeria	71
Rest of North Africa	51
Egypt	44
Rest of West Africa (Commonwealth)	28
Other Africa	29
Total world	*23746*

Expenditure (£m)

Total Europe	*5847*
France	671
Germany	976
Irish Republic	629
Netherlands	376
Belgium/Luxembourg	273
Italy	495
Spain	359
Sweden	256
Switzerland	301
Norway	190
Denmark	119
Austria	123

Israel	157
Poland	63
Greece	135
Portugal	97
Czech Republic	40
Russia	110
Finland	70
Turkey	69
Hungary	21
Yugoslavian States	30
Iceland	16
Rest of Europe	271
Total Northern America	*2370*
USA	2068
Canada	302
Total Central and South America	*305*
Brazil	95
Argentina	55
Mexico	29
Venezuela	8
Other Central and South America	65
Total Asia Pacific	*2134*
Japan	553
Australia	469
Hong Kong	166
India	130
New Zealand	105
South Korea	67
Malaysia	94
Thailand	107
Singapore	91
Rest of South East Asia	99
Pakistan	92
Taiwan	76
China	38
Other Asia Pacific	47

Total Middle East	*618*
Gulf States	341
Saudi Arabia	189
Iran	17
Other Middle East	71
Total Africa	*611*
South Africa	199
East Africa (Commonwealth)	129
Nigeria	99
Rest of North Africa	49
Egypt	60
Rest of West Africa (Commonwealth)	40
Other Africa	35
Total world	*11885*

Source: *International Passenger Survey*, Central Statistical Office;
Irish Republic figures supplied by Central Statistics Office in Cork

Market overview

Europe

Two thirds of all overseas visitors to the UK come from Europe. The overall number of visitors from Europe is increasing, particularly on short breaks. A weaker pound, the Channel Tunnel and cheaper air and sea fares have been major factors in this growth, which looks set to continue.

Around half of the world's outbound travellers come from Europe so the potential for growth is excellent, even though a different approach may be required to target each individual European country.

The European Travel Commission predicts that Europe's over-55 population will increase by 10 per cent between 1990 and 2000 to account for a third of the population as a whole. This group of people is now living longer and has higher disposable income so is likely to increase the volume of domestic and international travellers.

The Americas (USA, Canada and Latin America)

The largest proportion of visitors from the Americas come from the USA. This is the UK's most important market, in terms of visitor numbers and revenue. The population of North America is expected to grow by over 12.5 per cent from 276 million to 311 million between 1990 and 2010. Only around 13 per cent of the country's population have been to the UK so there is significant potential for growth, although the USA is also a volatile market. Visitor numbers from the USA can fall dramatically as a result of a weak dollar, fears of terrorism and economic recession.

The European Travel Commission predicts that the senior market in the USA and Canada will be particularly important. In the USA the senior market is the fastest growing segment of travel demand: the over-55s represent 21 per cent of the population and account for 28 per cent of all overseas trips.

In recent years there has also been record growth in visitor numbers and income from Canada and Latin America.

Asia Pacific

The Far East markets are growing rapidly, with Japan remaining the key source of tourism for Britain. Thailand, South Korea, India and Taiwan are expected to generate increasingly high numbers of international travellers.

Asia offers significant potential for growth, as two-thirds of the world's population live there. High economic growth is generating a growth in outbound travel from Asia at around 15 per cent per annum, whereas the world average is only 7 per cent. The youth market is particularly important in Asia.

Japan is currently the third most important generator of spending on international travel in the world. The trend for the Japanese has been to visit several European countries in one trip, although single country stays are becoming more popular as people travel to Europe for a second or third time. Segments offering potential include: female office workers; honeymooners, students (who are much more high-spending than European students) and 'silver-haireds'.

Africa and the Middle East

Visitor numbers from Africa are currently increasing slightly, but revenue has not been high. However, it is in Africa and the Middle East that the world's population growth is at its highest. South Africa is regarded as offering the strongest potential for growth in tourism to Britain. Prospects are also good for the Middle East where tourism to Britain is growing steadily and there has been a good increase in revenue.

Summary of market potential

Markets offering immediate potential for growth are: Europe, the USA, South Africa, Japan, Taiwan, South Korea and South East Asia.

Markets offering medium term potential are: Australasia, Latin America and Russia.

Market segments offering potential are:

▨ ageing populations in Europe, North America and Japan;

▨ youth – especially the special interest and activity segments;

▨ ethnic and VFR traffic;

▨ business travel – conferences, trade fairs, incentives, business study and extended business trips;

▨ English language study;

▨ 'green tourism'.

Marketing overseas

Before undertaking any overseas marketing you should consider the following points:

Should you undertake overseas marketing now?

Business from overseas markets will take time to materialise and pay off. It is generally better to establish a strong domestic business base before commencing overseas marketing. You must also be certain that you have adequate time and resources to dedicate to it.

Is your product suitable for overseas markets?

Not all products are appropriate for overseas markets and few products are suitable for every market and segment. The best ways of determining whether your product is suitable are to consider whether you already have any visitors or guests from overseas and to obtain relevant information from the British Tourist Authority.

If you already attract some overseas visitors, the implication is that you have a suitable product and could attract more. If you do not, it could be simply because overseas visitors are not aware of your product – more research will be necessary.

Which markets will you target?

It is essential to select a small number of overseas markets and segments, rather than trying to sell to everyone – unless you have a huge budget and product of mass appeal. You will need to obtain more information about relevant markets, by speaking to the BTA or reading their market guides.

Overseas marketing can be very expensive but need not be if you target markets carefully and appropriately. Make sure you understand the needs and characteristics of your chosen target markets.

How are you going to market your product overseas?

Very few products can be marketed totally independently. Partnership promotions are usually more successful and cost-effective. Depending on your product and region, you may choose to:

▧ work with a regional or area tourist board or company;

▓ work with a group of organisations from your area;

▓ work with similar products or types of businesses, which may also operate in other areas of the country. For example, hotels might join a hotel marketing consortium, or visitor attractions form an association with other similar attractions; or

▓ work directly with the BTA as part of one of their themed campaigns.

The benefits of partnership marketing are considerable and include:

▓ greater impact, particularly in markets where the individual products or areas are not well known;

▓ reduced costs;

▓ wider range of activities than would be possible for a lone organisation.

BTA activities in overseas markets

BTA has only limited resources available for promotion so it focuses on the strongest markets. It has undertaken extensive market research to identify key market segments in each country which offer the greatest potential for growth and financial reward. Strategic and tactical promotions and campaigns are developed for each market, usually under umbrella themes.

Britain already has an established reputation for its heritage, tradition, countryside and culture. In order to develop a new generation of visitors the BTA is now undertaking more innovative campaigns such as the 'Style and Design' initiative to position Britain also as a contemporary and stylish destination which will appeal to younger visitors as well as older ones. By creating a more vibrant image, the BTA will also be able to promote Britain's fashion, design, nightlife, restaurants and pop music.

BTA has developed expertise in the area of overseas marketing, so staff have good and specialist knowledge of the markets with which they deal. Whichever approach you use for overseas marketing activities it is likely that some of them will involve the BTA, who can offer both advice and a range of promotional opportunities.

The following describes some of BTA's main activities and promotional opportunities. A free guide, *How to Reach Your Overseas Customer – Working with BTA*, is available from the London office. Promotional activities for each market are described in more detail in another BTA publication, *Marketing Opportunities*, which is published annually.

The 'desks'

A large part of overseas activities take place within the network of overseas offices themselves, although they are usually co-ordinated by the London office. In London there are seven 'desks' with responsibility for a number of overseas countries divided up by area. Marketing executives at these desks provide the first point of contact for marketing activities within their regions. The regions are:

▓ Northern Europe;

▓ Southern Europe;

▓ Scandinavia;

▓ Central and Eastern Europe and Eastern Mediterranean plus Republic of Ireland;

▓ North and South America;

▓ All Asia, Japan, Australia, New Zealand;

▓ Middle East, Africa and Turkey.

In some cases it is still necessary to speak directly with the overseas offices. They obviously have more detailed experience of each market, but the London 'desks' are a useful starting-point from which you can obtain initial information about your chosen markets.

Market Guides

The BTA publishes a series of nearly 30 *Market Guides*, which are available individually or as a set. Each of the guides focuses on a specific country or area and includes:

▓ a cultural review;

▓ market summary;

▓ information about the travel trade structure and contact details;

▓ data on visitor numbers and expenditure;

▓ identification of key market segments and the activities BTA will be organising to target them;

▓ general information about doing business with that country/region.

Each of the *Market Guides* costs between £10 and £20 and is available from the BTA in London.

Press activities

The BTA Press Office provides regular feature articles, news stories and photographs to over 1000 overseas newspapers, magazines and correspondents. A monthly newsletter *Britain Calling* includes around 40 stories on new developments, forthcoming events and special interest activities.

The BTA retains editorial control over the material which it provides to overseas media contacts, selecting stories and information which it considers most newsworthy and appropriate. It is worthwhile sending your press information to the BTA Press Office for possible inclusion. Events information should be submitted at least (but preferably much longer than) three months in advance.

Press visits are another important aspect of the BTA's activities targeting the media. Journalists from the press, radio and television are invited to experience different aspects of Britain first-hand. Some journalists visit as part of a general promotion or on themed itineraries such as one covering the arts or gardens. Offers to host overseas journalists should be made to the press office.

Familiarisation visits

The BTA also organises a programme of familiarisation visits for tour operators and travel agents so they can gain more detailed information about different aspects of Britain. Each programme is different and may cover specific themes or regions. If you would like to be considered for inclusion in a familiarisation visit, you will need to offer complimentary services or discounted rates. Contact your regional/area tourist board or the travel trade department at the BTA.

The BTA tries to select journalists and tour operators as carefully as possible, to avoid 'freeloaders'. To gain maximum benefit from familiarisation and press visits follow-up contact is important. Press and familiarisation visits can take time to show rewards but are an important method of promoting facilities to overseas contacts who can influence others.

Exhibitions

Taking a stand at an overseas exhibition can be very expensive and individual organisations seldom make the same impact as those which join together to take a larger stand, themed by either a geographic area or type of facility. The BTA takes stand space at numerous consumer and trade exhibitions overseas.

Organisations wishing to participate under the BTA umbrella usually need to have been in business for at least two years. It is important to plan and book early, particularly for larger exhibitions such as the ITB in Berlin. The marketing executives on the individual 'desks' will be able to tell you about exhibitions within their particular territories and help you to decide which ones are most appropriate.

Try to speak to people who have taken stands at those exhibitions in previous years, because the profile of visitors and format for exhibitions varies enormously. Some exhibitions are only suitable for organisations with established overseas contacts, whereas others are useful for those which are just beginning.

The BTA also organises overseas workshops and sales missions, offering an opportunity to make direct contacts with the travel trade. These can be quite expensive, but it is sometimes easier to build contacts in this way and to make an impact by working together with a variety of organisations on a sales mission, even if the group includes your competitors. The workshops and sales missions are useful for the first venture into a new market, and need to be followed up with individual sales activities and direct mail to maintain contact.

Publications

The BTA publishes numerous leaflets, guides, maps and magazines for the public and trade in which it is sometimes possible to advertise or obtain editorial coverage. Some publications cover specific themes and campaigns whereas others focus on regions of Britain. Recent print campaigns have included activities such as walking, shopping, historic houses and gardens, golf and themes like 'style and design'.

More general publications include:

▦ the monthly magazine, *In Britain* (paid-for circulation);

▦ the annual *Britain Guide*, which is produced in 18 different languages and 27 geographic editions, tailor-made for particular overseas markets;

▦ *Family Days Out;*

▦ *Getting about Britain*;

▦ *UK The Guide,* a magazine for the youth market;

▦ *Agents Sales Guides*, for distribution to travel agents in certain markets.

Other services

Other BTA services cover specific aspects of overseas marketing (most of which incur a fee) such as:

▦ direct mail lists for hire;

- annual travel trade forum in London which includes presentations about the states of various overseas markets, followed by workshops where participants have an opportunity to present your product to BTA overseas managers;

- help with translations;

- photographic library with over 400,000 transparencies available for hire.

Further details of overseas marketing activities and publications can be obtained from:

British Tourist Authority
Thames Tower
Black's Road
Hammersmith
London
W6 9EL
Telephone: 0181 846 9000
Fax: 0181 563 0302.

Choosing overseas markets to target

You will need to identify a limited number of overseas markets. If you are marketing overseas for the first time, it is best to choose those countries from which you already receive visitors. Further choices should be based on:

- level of market potential and revenue as described above;

- propensity to visit your area;

- the level of interest which the chosen nationality has in the products you offer.

BTA has identified key characteristics for major overseas markets, which are outlined below. Further details about each nationality are published in the series of *Market Guides.*

Australia and New Zealand

▓ Australians are more likely to stay in Scotland, Wales and all regions outside London than the average overseas visitor.

▓ They enjoy visiting cultural attractions including castles, gardens and historic houses and plan their trips in detail.

▓ Most Australians come from New South Wales (around 38 per cent) and New Zealanders from Auckland (around 40 per cent).

▓ Australians and New Zealanders enjoy canal cruising and the countryside, and young New Zealanders are also often interested in tracing their ancestors.

▓ They are unlikely to complain and dress casually. All are environmentally conscious.

▓ Britain is their third most popular destination after New Zealand and the USA. Both stay longer than the world average (Australians: approximately 23 nights; New Zealanders: 22 nights; world average: 10 nights), so spend more per visit but less per day.

Belgium and Luxembourg

▓ Flemish speakers find Britain more appealing than French speakers, with the top five areas of interest being London, Scotland, scenery, historic towns and speaking English.

▓ Short breaks are becoming a year-round attraction, especially in the south east, and business travel is also important (approximately 30 per cent compared to the world average of 24 per cent).

▓ Visitors from Belgium (39 per cent) are interested in green tourism.

▓ Visitors from Belgium and Luxembourg enjoy a wide range of interests including cultural attractions (historic places 60 per cent, museums 57 per cent, theatre, ballet, opera and concerts 30 per cent), golf, walking and cycling.

Canada

- Family ties and theatre are the main reasons for travelling to Britain off-season.

- On average Canadians have a greater knowledge of Britain than Americans, and seek new experiences rather than traditional sites.

- Over 50 per cent of visitors from Canada are from Ontario, and over half of the total number of Canadians visiting Europe come to Britain.

- Canadians who visit Britain are older than the average visitor from overseas (30 per cent are over 55).

- Seven million Quebecois prefer France as a destination, but other than the shared language, links are weak and the cultural heritage of the UK continues to draw visitors.

- Canadians spend less per visit/day than the average world visitor.

France

- Forty-two per cent of French visitors are under 25 compared with the world average of 27 per cent.

- They come to Britain for its eccentricity, cosy pubs, bed and breakfasts, traditions, heritage, art galleries, museums, golf, music, arts, sport and country pursuits.

- Mountains, countryside and cities have become more attractive to the French in recent years than sun and snow.

- Britain is losing its image of a place where the weather and food are unreliable. A recent article in the French newspaper *Le Monde* even admitted that London is becoming one of the gastronomic capitals of the world.

- Britain's influence on the young through the music and fashion industry is increasingly recognised.

- Britain and Ireland is now the sixth most popular destination after Spain, Portugal and Italy, Germany and Austria.

Germany, Austria and Switzerland

▓ Visitors are growing bored of sun, sand and sea and looking towards destinations which can offer individuals an enriching, intellectual experience. They seek scenery, friendly people, quality accommodation, value for money and peace and quiet.

▓ Visitors are attracted to the culture, the countryside, a chance to practise their English, healthy activities and self-improvement.

▓ Half the visitors start planning their visit nine months in advance, and a quarter six months in advance.

▓ Britain is the sixth most popular destination of the Swiss after France, Spain, Italy, Austria and Germany.

▓ The Swiss are the wealthiest visitors per capita.

Greece

▓ As many as 50 per cent of visitors come to Britain for medical care, which partly accounts for a relatively high spend per trip.

▓ London's shopping draws as many visitors as minor surgery, but little interest is shown in historic buildings, museums and theatre.

▓ Day trips to places such as Windsor, Oxford and Bath, and coach trips to Scotland, are of limited interest.

Hong Kong

▓ The average visitor likes to do and see a lot and enjoys shopping and bargain hunting, but does not like walking (10 minutes maximum), the rain, the cold and they may miss Chinese food.

▓ Famous attractions and pageantry are of prime interest, along with the countryside. They are willing to venture outside London.

▓ Visitors are often quite loud, especially when in groups.

▨ They are generally quite flexible visitors, and do not plan in advance.

▨ Travel is popular with everyone, including those on relatively low incomes, as they are big savers.

▨ Favourite destinations include USA, Canada, Australia, Britain and New Zealand.

▨ Visitors from Hong Kong stay longer than average, and spend more per visit and per day.

India and Pakistan

▨ Top attractions such as Madame Tussaud's, the Changing of the Guard, and the Tower of London are of interest, as well as shopping for British brands.

▨ Visits are heavily concentrated on London, though other well-visited cities are Birmingham, Liverpool, Nottingham, Leicester, Bradford, Manchester, Oxford and Cambridge.

▨ Close historical ties between India and Britain mean the visitors are familiar with the English language, British culture and cricket. Most visitors are under 40 (45 per cent), quite well-off, and among a growing number of independent travellers, although business travel is increasing.

▨ Two-thirds of visitors from Pakistan are male independent travellers and 45 per cent of the total are visiting friends and relatives.

▨ Visitors from India and Pakistan react better to verbal explanation than print or written signs.

Ireland

▨ The majority of holiday and business travel is by sea in summer to Wales, the West Country, the North West and Scotland.

▨ They are attracted because the range of facilities, especially all-weather ones, is better than that found in Ireland.

▨ Short breaks to London, including the theatres, are also popular.

▨ Culture and heritage appeals to older, middle-class visitors who have already travelled extensively in the UK, and who visit historic sites, cathedrals, universities, theatres and concert halls.

▨ The Irish Republic is the fourth biggest generator of visits to Britain, and the third most lucrative in the world (although spend per day and length of stay is just below average).

Israel

▨ Britain has been a favourite destination for many years, and London is so well known it needs little advertising. Edinburgh is the second most popular city (thanks to the festival).

▨ Visitors are keen on culture, museums and art galleries, and especially interested in theatre (many visit the theatre every night of their stay).

▨ Spend per day is higher than average.

Italy

▨ An off-season visit to Britain is now more appealing than ever to Italians from Lombardy in the industrial north (47 per cent), Lazio (Rome and its region).

▨ When travelling to London, shopping is the main motivation. If outside London, Italians seek pleasant surroundings, experience of a different way of life, visits to famous places and pursuit of cultural interests.

▨ Scotland draws a disproportionate number of visitors (after London) because of its image of greenness, friendliness and simplicity.

▨ The visit is likely to be a second break.

▨ Visitors stay longer and spend more per day than average.

Japan

▨ Over 100 countries are touting for the tourist trade from Japan, so competition for Britain is fierce (France and Italy both attract more visitors than Britain, though Britain's growth since 1987 has not been bettered by any other major European destination).

▨ Visitors are often young and may be studying English, and include some of the 95 per cent of newly-weds who honeymoon overseas. Other visitors include office ladies in their 40s, reluctant to give up on their taste for foreign travel, and the growing silver market (Japan has the longest life expectancy in the world).

▨ Visitors want to observe culture, daily life and history, moving from visual tours to journeys of experience. Britain's historic buildings have a powerful pull (including pubs, shops, hotels and manor houses) as Japan's buildings are rarely older than 50 years.

▨ Visitors have a very high spend per day.

Latin America

▨ Visitors are most likely to come from Brazil (34 per cent) or Argentina (24 per cent).

▨ London is the most popular destination (seen as the capital of fashion by style conscious visitors), but a fondness for whisky means they are also aware of Scotland. Other city destinations include Cambridge, Bath, Stratford, York and Oxford.

▨ Leisure visitors are interested in theatre, museums and art galleries, and shopping (imported goods are still seen as an expensive novelty in many countries and the quality and variety of British products impresses).

▨ Argentineans also visit for sports (especially rugby), studying English, trade fairs and exhibitions. Fifteen per cent are business travellers and 10 per cent visiting friends and relations.

▨ Shorter staying Argentineans have an impressively high daily spend.

Scandinavia

▨ Visitors believe Britain to be warm and friendly, enjoy our sense of humour and liveliness (as seen on their TV), like the lifestyle which they think of as being typified by visits to the pub, and are all more comfortable with the English language than other European languages.

▨ Visitors have a fondness for golf and make an estimated 50,000 golfing trips per year.

▨ Danes have a good knowledge of British geography and customs, and Norwegians enjoy outdoor pursuits such as canal cruising.

▨ Norwegians dislike being taken for Swedes, and despite their good English appreciate a few words of greeting to be offered to them in their language when they visit their favourite destinations of Northumbria, Yorkshire, Humberside, Scotland and London.

South Africa

▨ South Africans are likely to visit Scotland, Wales and all English regions.

▨ For some South Africans, London's scale is overwhelming, but countryside, sport, castles, gardens and a sense of personal security are all strong draws.

▨ Cultural differences are not a problem and a few chilled beers in the fridge are much appreciated!

▨ Forty-eight per cent of visitors come from Transvaal despite recession and political instability.

▨ Britain vies with Namibia and Zambia as the most popular destination, but stays top of the league as a long-haul destination.

▓ South Africans (even with only distant British origin) retain strong links and long-haul travelling Afrikaners are more likely to visit Britain than any other country. The travel market is predominantly white.

▓ South Africans are keen to tour and their average length of stay is around 20 nights.

Spain

▓ London is the most favoured destination as it is seen as a fashion leader and has many markets.

▓ Scotland is increasing its appeal to the romantic Spanish imagination.

▓ Ideal holidays for Spanish people include lots of local colour and are packed with activities such as shopping, playing and watching sports, theatre, music and exhibitions.

▓ Nightlife, pubs and eating out are of prime importance – the Spanish like to eat late and stay out till the early hours. British cakes and desserts have a strong appeal.

▓ Spanish visitors tend to travel in groups and enjoy opportunities to meet and mix with locals. For this reason most prefer the family atmosphere of a country bed and breakfast or the bustle of city life.

▓ Half of all Spanish visitors to Britain are 34 or under, and Spanish visitors are generally fairly affluent city dwellers (30 per cent are from Madrid).

▓ Britain is the third most popular holiday destination after Portugal and France.

USA

▓ American visitors are more likely than average to be first-time visitors so London has a strong appeal, but American visitors also enjoy Yorkshire, Scotland and Wales.

▓ American visitors to Britain tend to be more affluent, better educated and older than the average American.

▓ Americans are drawn to Britain for its history and culture, shared heritage and language, friendliness and safety, ease and convenience of public transport and charm.

▓ Favourite activities are sightseeing on foot and taking photographs, shopping and seeing a show, visiting historic houses, castles, cathedrals, museums and galleries, touring the countryside by car or train.

▓ Britain remains the number one European destination – in reality and aspiration – but France and Germany represent increasing competition for the American dollar.

2

DEVELOPING A MARKETING PLAN

WHAT IS MARKETING?

As every marketing student learns, marketing is essentially about the four 'Ps', which stand for: product, price, place and promotion. Marketing is basically about selling the right product at the right price to carefully targeted people, using the best possible and most appropriate methods.

It is useful to be aware of the four 'Ps' and what they mean, but they should always be considered as an integral part of the planning process, rather than taken in isolation.

The *product* is what you are selling, not just its features but also how it is different or better than competitors' products. In marketing terms, services are also referred to as 'products' even though they may not be tangible. For simplicity's sake this book does the same.

In the tourism industry the product is often a complex mix of different services and products, which it might be better to regard as an 'experience'. For example, a sightseeing tour will include numerous components such as the coach and driver, guide's commentary, view from the coach window, entrance to visitor attractions and refreshments. Even a supposedly straightforward one-night stay in a bed and breakfast is made up of several components, ie the warmth of welcome, location, comfort and style of the bedroom and bathroom, and quality of the breakfast.

The *price* obviously refers to the actual price of the product, as well as commission structures and discounts, etc.

The *place* sometimes causes confusion as it does not relate to the place you are promoting, but the marketplace or the distribution channels through which your potential customers can buy your product, actually experience it or find information out about it.

Promotion is more straightforward and refers to the message and tools you will use to promote your product, such as PR, print material, direct mail, or advertisements.

The four Ps should become part of a carefully considered marketing plan, which you have taken the time to think about and jot down, even if only roughly. You will find that some of the tasks which initially seem laborious save you time later because you use the findings repeatedly. This is particularly true of aspects such as identifying your key strengths and the benefits you can offer.

Why take the time to actually plan and write down step-by-step what you are going to do and how?

▓ Marketing is essentially a process, rather than a series of scattered and isolated activities.

▓ Planning focuses your attention and gives you the opportunity to set targets. It means you will be able to develop better methods of evaluating results so you do not spend money unnecessarily.

▓ It may be necessary to reorganise your company or organisation's structure, once you have taken the time to plan your marketing, or at least to communicate to other staff what you plan to do so you are all 'pulling in the same direction'.

▓ It is important to schedule and co-ordinate all marketing activities so as to make them more effective and to save money. For example, if you are placing advertisements, that is often a good time to increase your PR activities.

ELEMENTS OF A MARKETING PLAN

Marketing plans should ideally include:

▓ *Current situation – what are you doing?* This should include a brief review of the 'product' you offer, analysis of your target markets, and any important trends.

▓ *Marketing objectives*. This will involve setting some basic targets and defining what you want to achieve.

▓ *Swot analysis*. A consideration of the factors which are likely to make you succeed or fail, looking both inside and outside your organisation.

▓ *Competitor analysis*. You will need to decide who your competitors are, what they are doing and how you can compete with them

▓ *Market research*. How much do you really know about your existing and potential customers? Before you can move forward you will need to establish basic information about them.

▓ *Target markets*. Consideration of which markets are most worthwhile and important to you.

▓ *Marketing tools*. For many the most interesting bit! You will need to develop a sort of shopping list of the promotional tools you will use and what budget you will devote to them.

▓ *Monitoring*. How will you know if you have been successful? You will need to decide how you are going to monitor your performance.

At the end of this section you will find a checklist so that you can make sure you have covered each of these areas in your marketing plan before looking in more detail at promotional activities.

You will probably find that as you work on one element of your marketing plan you think of aspects that are important to other elements, or that once you have developed one element, it means you need to go back and change some other sections. It is quite normal, and is actually the sign of a good marketing plan, which should be adapted as situations change, and constantly re-evaluated.

CURRENT SITUATION

This should not be a long section but should give an overview of three main areas: the 'product' you are trying to sell, current markets, and trends which might affect your business.

What are you selling?

A useful exercise is to consider the features, advantages and benefits of the 'product' or service you offer.

The *features* are physical characteristics. The *advantages* are offered by or included in the features and the *benefits* are what can be gained from those advantages. People buy benefits, not features.

Let us use the example of a hotel. When asked what sort of hotel they have, most hoteliers will respond by listing their features. Some might go on to explain the advantages of those features, but the ones who really attract guests are those who actually make the benefits more explicit. For example:

features:	20 bedrooms
advantages:	*en suite* facilities and quiet location
benefits:	rest, relaxation and privacy

Consider which hotel you would want to book. One whose brochure says, 'we have 20 bedrooms with private bathrooms, in a quiet countryside location' or one which says, 'you'll feel relaxed and refreshed, enjoying the fresh air and tranquillity at Hotel Bliss'?

Most tourism products are made up of several components which can be quite complicated. The key to success is selling *experiences* and *benefits* rather than features.

You need to spend a short time considering what you are selling so you can build on this.

Who are your current markets?

You should have a reasonable idea of who comes to visit your area or attraction, uses your services or books your accommodation. It is often easier to attract more of the same type of people than to attract completely new markets. This is because you know they already enjoy what you have to offer and presumably understand their needs.

Ask yourself the following questions:

▓ Where do your customers come from?

▓ How far do they travel to come to you?

▓ What is their average age?

▓ What sort of parties do they travel in – are they couples, families, small groups of friends or colleagues, tour groups, etc?

▓ How would you describe their income group and lifestyle?

▓ What are their interests?

▓ How do they book your product?

▓ Who/what influences their decisions?

▓ How did they hear about you?

If you find it difficult to answer these questions, you should make a note to conduct customer research as soon as possible.

What general trends might affect tourism and your business?

You should be aware of general trends such as:

▓ the state of the economy;

▓ economic and political changes overseas;

▓ markets which are growing or diminishing (the national

tourist boards and BTA publish useful surveys and research material on this);

▨ changes in leisure and holiday-taking habits, such as the increased trend towards independent travel, increase in the number of short break takers or increased demand for special interest holidays;

▨ technological developments, such as those in reservation systems or information technology like the Internet.

MARKETING OBJECTIVES

Marketing objectives should ideally include tangible targets, against which performance can be measured. For some tourism businesses such as tour operators or hotels, objectives are likely to be sales or profit-oriented. Marketing managers for destinations or tourist boards are more likely to set objectives relating to positioning or new product development.

When setting objectives it is important to be clear about how they will be measured and to set a clear timetable for monitoring effectiveness.

Objectives could:

▨ *be sales/profit-oriented*, eg to achieve a 10 per cent increase on sales over the next 12 months, or to increase a 20 per cent increase on current occupancy levels, by focusing on sales during the traditionally 'difficult' months of January and February;

▨ *relate to market share*, eg to achieve an increase of 5 per cent market share for UK activity holidays;

▨ *be about positioning*, eg to raise awareness of Bloggstown as a year-round romantic short break destination, by assisting Bloggstown tourism suppliers in the development and promotion of weekend packages;

You should try to ensure that your objectives:

▦ are measurable;

▦ include a time period for action so that you can monitor results;

▦ are realistic and in line with general market trends and demands.

CONDUCTING A SWOT ANALYSIS

Many organisations use a SWOT analysis as the first step in developing their marketing plan, perhaps because it is a relatively easy process! It is a useful audit and helps to focus the mind, but is only effective if followed up by consideration of the points it raises and actual plans on how to use the findings.

A SWOT analysis looks at the Strengths, Weaknesses, Opportunities and Threats facing an organisation or product.

The strengths and weaknesses relate to internal factors, some of which can be influenced or changed. The opportunities and threats are external factors, which often cannot be changed.

Once you have conducted a SWOT analysis you will be able to consider how you can make the most of the strengths and opportunities you have identified, and what you can do to minimise the weaknesses and threats. These findings should be integrated into the marketing plan.

Here are some of the aspects you should be looking at. Do not just restrict yourself to looking at these points. Using a team approach and 'brain-storming' together is a useful way of conducting a SWOT analysis – write everything down and think about it later. You may find that some things which you consider to be strengths could also be seen as weaknesses.

Strengths

▦ Your location – is it easily accessible, convenient, obvious and simple to find?

▦ Staff – are they professional and friendly, or do they have some special skills such as languages which make you superior to your competitors?

- Service – do you offer a good level of service or comfort or perhaps an unusually broad range of services?
- Marketing – do you have a high profile, strong established market, or use innovative marketing methods?

Weaknesses

- Your location – perhaps it is the reverse of the above?
- Reputation and image – could it be better?
- Staff – do they need more training or perhaps you have staff shortages?
- Services – could they be more efficient or better in some way?
- Internal problems – such as bad organisation or reactive instead of proactive management.

Opportunities

These are external factors such as:

- Trends or fashions – for example increased interest in certain activities such as golf or walking.
- Changes in population – such as more senior citizens living longer, with greater disposable income.
- Developments – perhaps technological changes like the expansion of the Internet.
- Promotional opportunities – such as activities organised by the BTA, targeting a particular market.

Threats

- Competition – what are your competitors up to? Perhaps there are some new developments which might affect your business?

▨ Economic effects – such as a recession, high inflation or unemployment.

▨ Developments – changes may be negative as well as positive.

Section Four gives an example of the SWOT analysis and recommendations which were developed for the county of Wiltshire.

COMPETITOR ANALYSIS

When you are involved in the day-to-day management of a business it is easy to think there is not enough time to watch what your competitors are up to. It is worth making the time. You can save time and money by keeping a keen eye on their activities, learning by their successes and failures.

There are two phrases which are often used (over-used) in tourism promotions: 'unique' and 'something for everyone'. As the chapter on promotional print explains, you need to think carefully about the words you use to describe your product.

It could be argued that almost every tourism product is 'unique' in some way; or even that none of them are. Whatever the case, 'unique' has become fairly meaningless and it is more effective to explain exactly what you mean.

'Something for everyone' assumes that the public are ready to fall in with the general masses, and take pot luck. Few of us are so easy to please that 'something for everyone' appeals. Most people are more likely to react to a more specific appeal.

The key is to find ways of differentiating yourself from your competition. Finding a competitive advantage means finding how you can compete more effectively. This relies on offering your customers something which is better than your competitors, either in real terms or through good marketing. You cannot do that unless you know what your competitors are doing.

A good way of doing this is to make a telephone enquiry and request information to be sent to you (if you think they might recognise your name you could use a different one and a friend's address) or to visit some of your competitors.

Remember, not all your competitors will be in the immediate locality. Some of them will be in other areas but can be considered as competitors because your consumers will make a choice between their establishment and yours. Whenever possible tour operators need to see their competitors' brochures and know what sort of products are on offer.

It helps if you make a conscious effort to carry out a fairly formal analysis every few months, jotting down your findings so you can decide how you will use the information.

Here are some of the things you should consider:

First impressions

How do they answer the telephone? Quickly and politely or as if it is too much effort?

What does their signage and entrance look like – how do their customers perceive them?

Pricing

Do they offer value for money? Does their pricing position them in a different way to you? How do they present their prices? Remember that you do not necessarily have to be the cheapest to compete more effectively. Some people are put off by prices which appear too cheap – value for money is more attractive.

Promotional material

If you asked for some information to be sent to you, how long did it take? Is the information complete? Could you learn from the format or design? Keep a look out for places where your competitors' literature is on display – should yours be there too?

Who are their customers?

If it is possible to actually see their customers you can learn a lot about them by assessing their age groups, people they are travelling with (for example do you see a lot of family groups or single people?) cars, clothes etc. Another way is to look at their promotional material, whether it is a leaflet or advertisement and try to decide to whom they are trying to appeal.

Is this exactly the same market as yours or a different one? If it is the same one, you can compete by learning more about your customers and what they want and ensuring your promotional activities convey this message. If your competitors attract a different market, should you target it too?

Their marketing activities

Few of us would recognise the difference between standard grocery products bought at two different supermarkets. It is the image and marketing of the supermarkets which makes the difference. In the same way you may find that your competitors are offering very similar products to you but marketing them differently.

Look out for any of their advertisements, even if they are only to recruit staff – you can learn a lot from them, by the way they present themselves. At exhibitions make sure you check out your competitors' stands and train yourself to look out for any information about them in the local or trade press.

When you have done all this you should be able to draw up a list of your closest competitors, looking at their prices, their welcome for visitors, facilities and promotional activities. Analyse each of these aspects and decide where you lag behind or are stronger. What are you going to do about it?

COMPETITIVE ADVANTAGE

What is your competitive advantage, ie your 'Unique Selling Point'? Most organisations find it hard to say immediately what marks them out from their competitors and how they are really different.

It is essential to try to define how you want to compete, in order to set targets and ensure that all your activities are focused on that aim.

According to Michael Porter's work* in the 1980s, there are basically three competitive strategies:

---

* Porter, M E (1985) *Competitive Advantage: Creating and Sustaining Superior Performance*, Free Press, New York.

▓ low-cost leadership;

▓ differentiation;

▓ focus.

As with many theories, it can be difficult to apply them to real-life situations in the tourism industry, but it is worth thinking about these three approaches and how you can use them. They are described below in an adapted format.

Low-cost leadership

A company can compete by keeping its costs down, so it can invest in better marketing or new product development to stay ahead of the competition, or as often happens, by keeping prices down and competing on price. This is possible for both large and small organisations. Large organisations can benefit from their mass purchasing power and economies of scale. Smaller operations such as guest houses can keep a tight control over their overheads and minimise costs.

Keeping control over costs does not always mean offering low prices – it might just mean more money becomes available for better marketing, to sell more and become even more profitable. Some companies do compete on price, but not always low prices. By developing a reputation for excellence, it is sometimes possible to demand higher prices. Remember the Stella Artois 'reassuringly expensive' advertisements?

Differentiated approach

As the name implies, a differentiated approach relies on having a 'unique' (in the original rather than promotional sense of the word!) product or offering a truly superior service, for which a higher price will often be charged. In the tourism industry, *reputation* goes a long way towards this, particularly in the case of five-star hotels. Most of them offer very similar services in a high-quality, polished environment, but the Savoy Hotel's reputation draws guests to it, rather than to its less well-established competitors.

Superficially, many guest houses and small hotels seem alike, especially in coastal resorts. They offer similar facilities and are often within a short distance of one another. How can they compete, if not on price?

Competing on price can be dangerous. Reduce your prices and at some point customers will either begin to suspect that you offer an inferior service or ask for further discounts. During the recession many hotels and attractions offered special discounts, accepted plenty of two-for-the-price-of-one vouchers and similar promotions. Some of these are losing their effect, because they have become so commonplace and customers cease to value the product at its *real* price.

Perhaps more than any other industry, tourism is not one which just relies on individual components. Most tourism products are made up of several inter-related ingredients, which together deliver a total *experience.*

A guesthouse may have the same number of bedrooms and basic services as its neighbour but is somehow made different by less tangible elements; ie the view from bedroom windows, pleasant garden, cosy lounge or warm welcome from the owners.

In this sense a differentiated approach is made possible. The basic elements of a tourism product or service may appear very similar but they can be brought together in different ways to develop an experience which is vastly different from competitors. This could mean a quicker service, one which is easier to book, an all inclusive price or warmer welcome.

For many companies using a differentiated approach, a strong brand image is essential, particularly where physical characteristics are almost indistinguishable. Airlines are a good example of this: they use the same type of aircraft to fly the same routes, often at quite similar prices, with the same basic services. However, they try to differentiate themselves from their competition by creating a strong brand image, investing vast sums of money to develop customer loyalty, brand recognition and appeal.

Even very small companies can make a bigger impact by creating a stronger brand. Always using the same logo and typeface on letterheads, brochures and signage all contribute to this.

The differentiated approach relies on excellent customer service and creative marketing to stay ahead of competitors. The most important factor is identifying key strengths and focusing on them.

Focused approach

A focused approach means concentrating on particular markets, understanding their needs completely and therefore developing products and promotions which are completely appropriate for those markets. This approach requires an excellent knowledge of the chosen markets, and insight to direct all marketing efforts precisely. It is equally important to anticipate changes in the marketplace as well as demands for new products and services.

A focused approach is often used by smaller companies without massive resources but with an excellent understanding of their target markets. Instead of using an 'all things to all people' or 'something for everyone' approach, they can operate within niche markets which are too small to attract the 'big boys'.

Smaller companies can develop closer and more direct relationships with their clients so a focused approach is particularly suitable. Concentrating on a limited number of markets is also more cost-effective.

In summary, there are many different ways of developing a competitive edge. You need to ask yourself:

▒ What makes your product/service better or different?

▒ What are the benefits of it to your customers?

▒ How are you offering exactly what customers need?

▒ Why should anyone buy your product/service more than that of your competitors?

Remember that the majority of tourism products are made up of many different elements. The 'product' is not just one thing, but a total experience which includes:

▓ physical characteristics;

▓ greeting and welcome;

▓ how people are treated during the 'experience', whether its a flight, a week's tour, an overnight stay or a visit to an attraction;

▓ how easy the location is to find and how accessible it is;

▓ how good is the food and the way in which it is served;

▓ other feelings such as those of security or comfort and relaxation;

▓ how closely the experience matches the promises of the promotional material.

MARKET RESEARCH

Marketing activities can involve spending considerable sums of money, without any guarantee of return on the investment. Good research will help you to find out more about your target markets, or even who they are. It will help you to decide what they like and dislike about your service, how it could be improved, and how it should be marketed. Research will even help you to decide whether or not you have spent your money wisely. Market research is a very useful tool which can be used for the following:

Product development

Changing or developing a new product or facility is potentially expensive. Market research can help to establish whether there is sufficient demand for new facilities or what sort of facilities you should develop. It can help to decide how the new facilities or service would be perceived, and even how much clients would be prepared to pay for them.

Sometimes more general research can lead to product development. The Tower Bridge Experience in London is an interactive exhibition within Tower Bridge, which includes a walk over the covered walkways at the top of the Bridge. They recently conducted a survey to find out what aspects of the exhibition visitors were particularly interested in.

A large proportion of the visitors surveyed replied that they thought the best feature of Tower Bridge was the opportunity to enjoy the view over the Thames from the glass walkways. As a result of this research Tower Bridge Experience now offers tour operators a 'quick tour' which bypasses the exhibition area and allows visitors just to enjoy the view from the walkways.

Test marketing

Instead of launching a new product or service on a large scale, test marketing can be used to gauge consumer reactions or to make final adjustments to the product or the way it is promoted.

Focus groups are frequently used for test marketing before launching major advertising campaigns. A small group of people corresponding to the target market are invited to give their comments and reactions to products or campaigns. A trained researcher shows the group photographs, videos or other visual material and then directs the discussion to find out more information about the group members' reactions.

When working on the development of a new attraction in the Midlands, consultants used focus groups to establish whether the public were interested in the general concept of the attraction and how it could be made more attractive, either by offering additional facilities or changing the way the attraction would be promoted.

The attraction was a forest-based project, designed to help the public enjoy and appreciate trees and woodlands. It was aimed at families so the focus groups used young children in 'friendship pairs' (so they would be less shy and more forthcoming with their comments) in one group and parents in another.

They were shown artists' impressions of the attraction and asked about their perceptions of forests and what they meant to them. At this stage it emerged that the public expected to see various woodland animals within the attraction, even though it was unlikely they would normally spot them in an ordinary forest. This aspect had been left out of the original concept. It was apparent that the public would be disappointed if the concept remained exactly as it was so consideration was given to developing the attraction to fit public perceptions.

Campaign development

It is useful to know how consumers will react to marketing activities. A major insurance company planned to launch a new type of mortgage, which their promotional material referred to as the 'red ribbon mortgage'.

Before doing so, panels of consumers were asked for their reactions to this 'strapline' and accompanying illustrations. Did they view it positively? How did it make them feel? In fact, the red ribbon mortgage promotion was changed. Market research showed that people associated red ribbons with red tape – not a good thing for a mortgage which was supposed to be less bureaucratic than others!

As well as finding out how people will react to a campaign, market research can help to assess the effectiveness of marketing activities. For example, a visitor attraction might conduct a survey to find out how people made the decision to visit. This would reveal information about the success of marketing initiatives as well as information about the visitor profile.

The London Tourist Board made extensive use of focus groups to develop a new brand mark for London and to work on its present marketing campaign. London Tourist Board's use of market research is described in Section Four.

Customer information

It is easier to target similar people to the ones who already visit you or use your services, than to target a completely new market. By developing a 'profile' of current customers, you can build a clearer picture of your primary target markets and decide how to approach them.

It is sometimes easy to assume that you know your current visitors well but a visitor or guest survey can help to improve your marketing activities. For example, Sussex may seem quite a long journey from Essex. Informal research at a privately-owned woodland gardens in Sussex found that with the opening of the Dartford Crossing many groups were starting to visit from Essex. When questioned about the aspects of the gardens they enjoyed most, one of the main responses was that they liked the undulating Sussex countryside, which is so different from the flatter Essex landscape.

This information enabled the gardens to stress the slightly hilly woodland landscape in their publicity material; and to choose exhibitions to attend in Essex from which their competitors were noticeably absent.

Customer satisfaction

Most tourism suppliers seek to ensure customer satisfaction – they want customers to return and spread positive word-of-mouth publicity. Surveys are a useful way of establishing customer satisfaction levels and finding out what improvements are necessary.

SURVEY METHODS

There are basically two different types of research: *qualitative* and *quantitative*.

Quantitative surveys seek specific answers which are often presented in statistical form, such as '25 per cent of visitors to London said they would return'. Quantitative surveys generate statistical information, answering questions such as who? where? and when?

Quantitative research is particularly useful for monitoring changes and development. For example, a hotel which wishes to conduct 'Welcome Host' training might decide to conduct a guest survey before and after the training session to try to gauge its effect.

Qualitative research seeks to find out people's personal reactions and feelings about products or experiences. It is particularly useful when developing marketing campaigns and for motivational research, asking why or how customers made the decision to purchase (or not purchase) certain products. Qualitative surveys can be more expensive because they require skilled interviewers and may take longer, but they do probe below the surface.

Research can be conducted on different levels, according to the detail and amount of original information required.

As the name implies '*desk*' or '*secondary research*' uses existing reports and published sources such as survey directories, reports and surveys to gather information and can be carried out within an office or library. The BTA library at Hammersmith, London contains a wealth of product and market information. It is possible to use the material there by making an appointment in advance and paying a small usage fee.

'*Primary research*' means actually developing questionnaires and going out into the 'field' to ask selected members of the public or trade for their response.

Should you conduct research in-house or use a specialist research agency?

You will need to decide whether you are going to conduct the research in-house or commission a specialist research agency. Some straightforward research can be conducted perfectly well by existing staff, providing you take the time to think questions through carefully. More detailed research, particularly involving focus groups or qualitative research requires a specialist approach and skills.

In-house research will usually be cheaper than employing an agency but do not underestimate the time it will take to develop the questionnaires, conduct interviews, analyse results and decide how to use them.

Using a specialist research agency will superficially cost more but the results will generally be more reliable and representative. If you need to interview specific market segments, using an agency is often a quicker route because they know exactly where to go to target those segments.

You can obtain a list of reputable research companies from the Market Research Society, or from your regional tourist board.

Market Research Society
15 Northburgh Street
London EC1
Telephone: 0171 490 4911
Fax: 0171 490 0608

Choosing a sample

It is important to determine the precise purpose of the research to choose the research method and sample. One of the keys to good research is having a sample (of responses) which are large and representative enough to help you take appropriate action. You will need to decide not just how large your survey sample should be but also how you will determine the survey sample.

- *Stratified sampling* divides the population into classes and draws a random sample of people from each of these 'classes'.
- *Cluster sampling* uses a group as a sample unit.
- *Judgement sampling* relies on the researcher's subjective opinions about the people they will call on to respond to the research questions.
- *Convenience sampling* uses people who are likely to have views on the subject matter of the research and who are readily available.

Large-scale research is not always necessary. For some purposes a representative sample of, say, ten people in a focus group might be sufficient. For others a much larger number and broader cross-section of people will need to be interviewed.

In order to interview a representative sample for your purposes you may need to decide key criteria such as age bands, economic status or geographic origin. If this is the case, then set some filtering questions at the beginning of your questionnaire to enable you to interview people only within the defined sample quotas.

It may also be necessary to stagger the research over a period of time, to take account of different visitor or guest profiles.

It is usual to 'qualify' the data obtained by questionnaires. This will ensure a representative sample and enable you to take any external influences into account. A 30-year-old married man will have a very different perspective to a 75-year-old widow.

Standard demographic questions can be used as filters. They determine:

- male/female;

- age: usually presented as age groups, rather than asking respondents to give their precise age, as some people would prefer not to do this;

- occupation or socio-demographic profile;

- marital status: single, married/cohabiting, previously married.

Socio-economic classification

Although the idea of a 'class' is becoming increasingly suspect, it is often convenient to be able to break down the population into groups. Since there is often a degree of correlation between occupation and life-style (the latter in turn having some influence on buying habits, etc), the classification now commonly used is based on occupation of 'head of household'. This classification was developed for the National Readership Survey.

Many people have reservations about the system but it is useful to know what the different categories represent:

A   Higher managerial administrative or professional
B   Intermediate managerial administrative or professional
C1 Supervisory, clerical, junior administrative or professional
C2 Skilled manual workers

D   Semi-skilled and unskilled manual workers
E   State pensioners, widows, casual workers and lowest grade
    earners

These classifications are usually simplified to: AB, C1, C2, and DE.

Formulating questionnaires

Before you start to develop a questionnaire you should note down your objectives for the research and answer these questions:

▓   Why do you want to carry out the research?

▓   Is the information already available elsewhere? Would secondary research be sufficient or do you need to use primary research?

▓   What are the issues you need to address?

▓   What size sample do you think will be necessary? Remember that not everyone you ask to respond will do so.

▓   What sort of people do you need within your sample to be truly representative?

▓   What is the best method for obtaining the information?

▓   Where should the research be carried out?

▓   When is the best time to carry out the research?

▓   How are you going to implement the results? Are you prepared to act on the results or are you only expecting certain responses?

The design of the questionnaire will determine the research's accuracy. Try to avoid questions which:

▓   are leading and make the respondent reply in a certain way, thus 'skewing' the results of the research;

- are too difficult to answer – these questions will probably lead to an educated guess rather than a real answer;

- are loaded or emotive so it is difficult to respond honestly;

- are ambiguous and do not offer clear answers;

- are too vague to stimulate a meaningful answer;

- use jargon so are difficult to understand;

- include two questions in one.

You should beware of making the questionnaire too long and making it into a memory test – only ask about recent decisions and experiences. You should also remember to explain the purpose of the questionnaire at the beginning and thank the respondent at the end.

Types of question

Close ended

Requiring a yes/no answer, ie 'Have you been on holiday?'

Open questions

Using words such as who, what, why, where, when to elicit more descriptive responses; please explain why you chose that destination?

Multiple options

How many weekend breaks do you take per year? Please tick one:

none	[ ]
one	[ ]
two	[ ]
three or more	[ ]

Differentiated scale

How much did you enjoy your meal? Please select one:

yuk   [ ]
OK   [ ]
quite good   [ ]
fantastic   [ ]

Differentiated scales are often used in questionnaires which seek to establish rates of customer satisfaction. Multiple option questions are particularly useful in postal questionnaires if you wish to keep the questionnaire simple and maximise response rates.

Research methods

There are several research methods which you could use, each with their own advantages and disadvantages:

Personal or face-to-face interviews

These enable you or a trained interviewer to meet the respondent and ask more detailed questions.

Advantages:

▒ interviewer can stimulate interest;

▒ interviewer can see and assess respondent to ensure correct interpretation of responses;

▒ enables items to be shown – such as pictures, lists of products or sample advertisements;

▒ facilitates deep probing to obtain more detailed information.

Disadvantages:

▒ high cost per interview;

▒ interviewer's attitude may influence response;

▦ requires trained interviewers, which can be expensive;

▦ fewer interviews per day, giving low response rate but more detailed information for each respondent.

Postal questionnaires

Advantages:

▦ relatively inexpensive;

▦ can easily cover large geographic areas;

▦ needs little skill to implement, although questionnaires must be carefully designed to ensure easy, unaided completion.

Disadvantages:

▦ response rate may be low and biased to extreme negative and positive views – offering some form of incentive to encourage responses by a given deadline will improve response rates;

▦ respondents often need reassurance that there will be no follow-up sales call.

Telephone interviews

Advantages:

▦ more economic than personal interviews;

▦ easy to cover large geographic areas;

▦ can record conversations or input responses directly into computer to produce fast results;

▦ achieves higher response than postal questionnaires.

Disadvantages:

▦ may be difficult to contact some people, so difficult to achieve quotas;

▨ daytime telephoning can be expensive;

▨ lacks the interaction of face-to-face interviewing.

Tips to make your research more successful

▨ Before you print hundreds of copies, test your questionnaire on friends and colleagues to see how easy it is to answer, and check that the responses will not be 'skewed' by the way you have set the questions. This is especially important for self-completion questionnaires because an interviewer will not be present to ask if a question does not make sense.

▨ If you use a multiple-choice format, it is useful to have a card for each question, on which you have printed the relevant responses. If you are asking questions about advertisements or brochures it is also useful to have examples to show the respondent so they do not need to rely on memory and can focus properly on giving accurate answers.

▨ Ensure you have sufficient time and funds to carry out useful research – research should be seen as an investment.

▨ Be willing to abandon your preconceived ideas if the research does not result in the findings you expected!

▨ Do not just carry out research once – it should be part of a regular programme of monitoring and evaluation.

▨ If you are not prepared to *use* the research findings, do not bother doing it. Implementation of recommendations is the only key to success.

IDENTIFYING TARGET MARKETS

The total market for tourism products is huge. It is made up of people looking for budget accommodation and rooms in exclusive country house hotels, of sun-worshippers and culture-vultures, of couch potatoes and ardent adventurers. You cannot hope to satisfy all of the people all of the time. Nor should you try to target all of them at once. Broadcast marketing, or trying a 'something for everyone' approach is expensive and rarely successful.

It is far more productive and cost-effective to identify several smaller groups of people or market segments. Segmentation means breaking markets down into a more manageable size, and gaining a precise understanding of different groups of people. Once you understand what each group needs and expects you can then choose which segments you are most likely to satisfy.

When choosing market segments you will need to ensure that they are:

▓ easily identifiable and distinct from the mass market;

▓ large enough to make targeting them worthwhile – you should also consider whether or not they are growth markets;

▓ easy to reach – either because they are geographically close to you or there are obvious and established channels of distribution and media through which you can target them.

Segments can be identified through numerous methods:

▓ *Age*: people choose different products according to their age and activities. However, this should not be the only criteria (see below).

▓ *Economic status*: for example budget accommodation providers will target people who are travelling on a restricted income.

▓ *Purpose of travel*: reason for travel and any special needs. For example, a business traveller will look for efficiency and prompt service whereas a family are more likely to look for fun activities.

▓ *Nationality*: as the section about overseas marketing indicates, some nationalities have a greater propensity to travel or indulge in certain activities than others. Once you have chosen specific nationalities or countries to target you will still need to define segments within that group.

▓ *Geographic location/origin*: for example, visitor attractions usually find that most visitors come from within one hour's travelling time from the place where they live or are staying.

▓ *Lifestyle, consumer attitudes and behaviour*: there are numerous studies and reports which break populations down into smaller subgroups according to aspirations, attitudes and general lifestyles. You may find it useful to use an existing classification or to develop one of your own. A relatively easy lifestyle analysis which helps you to picture a segment more clearly is to imagine 'a day in the life of...'.

Segmentation usually involves combining the above methods so you can develop a complete profile for different market segments. The more detail you can add about different segments the better. The total market for any product is likely to be quite wide, but by describing the differences between segments, it becomes possible to create focused and cost-effective strategies for each one.

Beware of simply identifying a segment such as 'old people'. Just because they are within a similar age group, people are not all similar. Within the general grouping of 'old people' there are many variations. For example:

▓ How old is old? Perceptions vary – a ten-year-old would suggest that 30 is already ancient!

▓ Income also varies – some 'old' people exist on state pensions, others are still working.

▓ How active are they? There is a world of difference between house-bound senior citizens and the village 'busy-body' who is at the heart of the community.

You should be able to identify a fairly long list of potential segments. It is useful to consider numerous markets and to prioritise them, dividing them into primary and secondary targets.

Primary targets will generally correspond to current client groups. These should ideally be segments showing good growth, which are fairly easy to target because you already know a lot about them and have been successful in attracting them.

Secondary markets may be more difficult to reach and represent a more long-term objective, but show excellent potential.

When prioritising market segments, there are three main questions to ask:

How attractive is the segment?

You will need to decide what 'attractive' means. This usually means that the segment is sizable, prepared to pay the market price for the product on offer, and fairly aware of the product.

How easy is the segment to reach?

Segments which are easy to reach are usually clearly defined, can be persuaded to not choose competing products, and can be reached through established and affordable media and distribution channels.

How much will it cost to reach the segment?

The deciding factor will often be the marketing budget. It is not possible to address every segment so it is essential to determine which ones will cost most money to reach and how accessible they really are. A sensible approach is to identify short and long-term markets.

When choosing target markets it is useful to note that segments will not all be equally aware of your product or ready to buy.

Every purchaser buying any product effectively goes through five key stages:

1. Unawareness
2. Awareness
3. Understanding
4. Conviction
5. Response

It is unusual for a potential buyer to move immediately from the stage of unawareness to response (ie 'purchase'), so they need to be 'moved' from stage to stage.

Promotional messages have to be delivered at all times to move visitors along from stage to stage. If this does not happen, they will move backwards. For example, a current hotel guest is at the response stage but when they go home, they could easily forget the hotel and never return again if they are not targeted.

The Table below shows the stages from 'unawareness' to 'response', and their relative potential, which will affect the choice of segments.

Purchasing Stages

Stage	Potential
Unawareness	Long-term possibility
Awareness	Medium-term return on investment
Understanding	Strong potential visitor
Conviction	Very likely to visit next year
Response	Current visitors

These stages and the promotional messages and methods which they each need are discussed in more detail in Section Three: Promotional Tools.

MONITORING AND EVALUATION

It is easy to become involved in the planning and implementation stages of marketing activities, without spending any time looking at the success of those activities and considering how they could be improved.

The marketing plan should include objectives and timescales, so you can build in a monitoring mechanism. It is important to set deadlines to evaluate performance. There are several ways of doing this:

▓ Compare actual performance annually against the objectives set.

▓ Measure bookings or requests for information and conversion rates weekly, monthly or quarterly – and look at periods of major marketing activity to see if they had the desired effect. This method will also help to clarify peak booking periods.

▦ Analyse sales and profits on a regular basis.

▦ Use market research to measure customer's awareness of advertising messages or similar promotions.

▦ Conduct market research to identify whether the customer profile has changed after particular marketing activities.

This list is by no means exhaustive. The important message is that the marketing plan should set specific dates and methods of evaluating progress and build in systems to re-evaluate at regular intervals. This will probably mean a rolling programme of research, analysis of marketing activities and product development.

CHECKLIST – MARKETING ACTION PLAN

Use the following checklist to make sure that you have thought about all aspects of your marketing plan.

Current situation

▦ What is the product or experience you are offering?

▦ What are the key benefits?

▦ Who are your current markets?

▦ What general trends might affect your business, negatively or positively?

Marketing objectives

▦ What objectives do you want your marketing plan to achieve?

▦ How will you know if it has been successful?

▓ What timescale and deadlines have you set?

SWOT analysis

▓ What are your strengths?

▓ What are your weaknesses?

▓ What opportunities do you have?

▓ What are the threats which you face?

▓ How can you maximise those strengths and opportunities?

▓ What can you do to minimise those weaknesses and threats?

Competitor analysis

▓ Who are your competitors?

▓ What do they offer?

▓ What are their prices and how do yours compare?

▓ What are their markets?

▓ How do they promote themselves?

▓ What are the relative advantages and disadvantages of their product compared to yours?

▓ How can you learn from them?

▓ Are there any opportunities you could exploit which they are missing?

Competitive advantage

▓ How are you going to compete?

▓ Do you need to invest more in marketing?

▓ Do you need to develop new products?

▨ Can you offer a product or experience which is truly different and better than your competitors?

▨ Can you focus on niche markets, whose needs you understand and can satisfy?

▨ What is your Unique Selling Point?

Market research

▨ What market research do you need to undertake?

▨ When and how often do you need to do it?

▨ How will you do it?

▨ What size of sample will you need?

▨ How do you plan to implement the results?

Target markets

▨ Which will be your primary markets?

▨ Which will be your secondary markets?

▨ Which market segments will you target?

▨ What do you already know about those markets?

▨ What do you need to find out?

For each market segment

▨ What is their level of awareness of your product?

▨ Do you need to adapt your product in any way?

▨ Do you need to adapt your pricing structure?

▨ What channels of distribution do they use – how will they access your product or make a booking?

▨ What channels of communication are most appropriate for that market?

▨ What promotional messages do they most want to hear?

Marketing tools

For each market segment you will need to select appropriate tools and messages.

▨ What tools will you use and how?

▨ Brochure and print material?

▨ Advertising?

▨ PR activities?

▨ Direct mail?

▨ The Internet?

▨ Exhibitions?

▨ Sales activities?

▨ Will you be able to work with a consortium?

▨ How will you work with the tourist boards?

▨ Will you need to employ consultants to do any of the work?

Monitoring

▨ What methods will you use to monitor the effects of your marketing activities?

▨ When will you do that?

▨ When will you review your marketing plan and develop a new one?

SAMPLE MARKETING PLAN – PORTOBELLO, LONDON

This is a marketing plan, written following the guidelines of the previous chapter, for the area of Portobello in London. It is by no means a comprehensive plan – more detail would normally be included in the section on marketing tools, as the plan is developed and refined. However this sample marketing plan should provide a useful outline for you to follow as you develop your own plan.

Current situation

This marketing plan is for a 'product' which is effectively both a destination and visitor attraction. The area of Portobello near Notting Hill in London, is famous for its antique market which takes place every Saturday and is one of the biggest in the world, attracting many thousands of Londoners and tourists each year. The Portobello Antiques Market enjoys an excellent reputation as *the* place to shop for antiques, and attracts affluent visitors from all over the world.

Not many people realise the true extent of the whole market, and that it does not just sell antiques or take place only on Saturdays. Portobello Road market actually stretches northwards toward Golborne Road and includes many other stalls as well as those selling antiques. Many of the stalls selling fruit and vegetables are there on weekdays, as well as a growing number selling bric-a-brac, and arts and crafts products on Fridays. The surrounding streets are also of interest to visitors, with an unusually wide range of specialist shops and quality bars and restaurants.

The North Kensington City Challenge Company was established to help bring about the economic regeneration of the Portobello area. One of its aims is to increase the numbers of high spending visitors to Portobello, stimulating more stall-holders, shops and restaurant owners to establish new businesses in the area.

Portobello offers visitors greater variety and interest than they have become accustomed to in increasingly homogeneous High Streets. The main challenge is to raise awareness of Portobello as an area, and not just the antiques market, and to encourage people to visit the whole market and surrounding streets on other days, as well as during the main market on Saturdays.

In so doing, there is an opportunity to attract more stall-holders and shop-keepers to create an even greater critical mass, in turn attracting more visitors.

Marketing objectives

The main marketing objective is to develop visitor numbers to the whole Portobello area throughout the week. Marketing activities will aim to do this by raising awareness of the wide range of facilities in the area and providing accurate information to help potential visitors decide to visit.

Very little information currently exists to indicate present levels of visitor numbers, so it will be difficult to actually ascertain the success of this initiative. Limited market research has been undertaken to date.

However, the market traders, shop and restaurant owners will be aware of increases in business, which it is hoped will be conveyed to the North Kensington City Challenge team. It is also expected that if the initiative is successful, there will be greater take-up of market stalls – this is something which the Portobello Market Office will be able to monitor.

The initiative will be ongoing. However, this marketing plan sets out activities which it should be possible to achieve within six months to one year, beginning to show positive results after about six months.

Swot analysis

The following are the main strengths, weaknesses, opportunities and threats for the Portobello area:

Strengths

▓   Well-known market, with an excellent reputation for antiques.

▓ Attracts visitors from all over the world.

▓ Good central location.

▓ Good transport links, on numerous bus routes, and close to Notting Hill Gate, Ladbroke Grove and Westbourne Grove underground stations.

▓ Amazing range and diversity – market (original atmosphere with the 'touters' and back slang); restaurants – food lovers' paradise.

▓ Notting Hill Carnival has put the area on the tourist map.

▓ Good general signage in the area – which is currently being improved.

Weaknesses

▓ Few visitors realise that the market extends north towards the Westway and sells a far greater range of products than just antiques.

▓ There is generally low awareness of Portobello as an area in which to shop (beyond the market) and eat, although nearby Notting Hill is becoming a fashionable place to eat and shop.

▓ Very limited parking.

▓ Can become overcrowded, particularly on Saturdays.

▓ Notting Hill and Portobello have a reputation among Londoners as a drug centre (although this is rapidly changing); and negative publicity about the Notting Hill Carnival may have reinforced the fear of violence in the area, even if this is over-stated.

Opportunities

▓ As the recession comes to an end, there is increased demand for interesting places in which to shop and eat.

▓ London is fast gaining an international reputation as a city in which to shop and eat – many of the aspects sought by visitors to Britain can be found in the Portobello area.

▓ Consumers are tiring of homogeneous High Street shops and restaurants and are increasingly looking towards more interesting specialist shopping areas, which Portobello offers.

Threats

▓ London has many other markets, which are all competing for the same market – Portobello will need to differentiate itself in order to compete effectively.

▓ Portobello does not enjoy such a strong reputation as some other more prominent shopping and eating areas.

Action points arising from the SWOT analysis

The following actions will be necessary to maximise these strengths and opportunities and to minimise the weaknesses and threats. *The main promotional activity will be to develop a strong identity for the Portobello area. This should:*

▓ build on the positive reputation of the antiques market, at the same time demonstrating the greater extent and facilities of the Portobello area;

▓ stress the excellent transport links and good signage in the area – easy to get to, easy to find;

▓ place particularly strong emphasis on the range and diversity of products sold in the markets and surrounding specialist shops and promote Portobello as a 'hot spot' for excellent bars and restaurants;

▓ encourage visitors to use public transport and visit at less busy times;

▓ stress that Portobello is different – some areas may have a slight 'edge' to them, but this is part of Portobello and its diversity and what makes it different from and more interesting than sterile High Streets in other areas.

Competitor analysis

Competitors to the Portobello area include other markets and other shopping and entertainment areas.

Other markets

Some of the markets with which Portobello is competing include:

▒ Camden Lock;

▒ Covent Garden;

▒ Spitalfields;

▒ other smaller and specialist markets.

Most of these markets are well-established and enjoy a strong reputation for various products, although none of them are as well-known for antiques. However, Camden Lock attracts many more young visitors, and is better established in overseas markets as a fashionable place to visit. Prices at each of the other markets vary according to the types of products on sale, but it is believed that prices in Portobello are competitive.

Several of the markets have developed entertainment programmes, using street performers to enhance and enliven their atmosphere. They are extensively promoted, using a combination of print material, entries in tourism publications and PR activities. Portobello needs to undertake similar activities in order to compete more effectively.

Other shopping and entertainment areas

Some of the shopping and entertainment areas with which Portobello is competing include:

▒ Oxford Street;

▒ Kensington;

▒ Covent Garden;

▒ Soho.

Each of these shopping and restaurant areas is well-established, and has a stronger reputation than Portobello, either as an entertainment district or general shopping area. However, most of them have a restricted selection of shops which can easily be found on most High Streets. Portobello has very few High Street chains, and offers a far greater range and diversity, as well as numerous 'quirky' shops and restaurants.

The visitor markets for these areas obviously vary, according to the products on sale, but are generally Londoners and some overseas visitors. The highest proportion of overseas visitors go to Camden Lock, and Central London areas such as Oxford Street and Covent Garden. Portobello enjoys a significantly high number of overseas visitors, predominantly to the antiques market.

The main opportunity for Portobello is to exploit the demand for interesting places to eat and shop. Overseas visitors are looking for quirky 'English' places, which do not resemble their own High Streets. Londoners are looking for interesting and exciting new places, and more interesting products than they are likely to find in standard shopping areas. They also enjoy the idea that they are going to 'new' areas which are becoming increasingly fashionable, rather than going to established tourist spots.

Competitive advantage

Portobello needs to use a differentiated approach, stressing that it has a truly different product to offer, which stands above other markets and shopping/entertainment areas. It needs to raise its profile with a strong branding and by stressing that visitors to Portobello will find an unusual and quirky mix of styles, products and people.

It needs to use this very diversity as its Unique Selling Proposition and stress the mix, acknowledging rather than camouflaging its reputation as being slightly 'on the edge', unlike many other areas which have become sterile and lost their identity.

At the same time there is a need to focus on the development of the 'product', for example by encouraging stall-holders and shops to sell unusual products, and by developing a street entertainment programme to add to the atmosphere of the market. This must be done in a sensitive way to avoid changing the 'feel' of the place and creating an artificial atmosphere.

Market research

There is a need to undertake more market research to find out more about existing visitors, and especially how they hear about Portobello. As promotional activities develop it would be useful to investigate their effectiveness (although it can take several months before many promotional activities begin to have an effect).

Primary research will be necessary, using face-to-face personal interviews. It would be useful to use street surveys which ask the same questions but at different times of the day and week. This should be done at least every three months so that seasonality can be assessed and direct comparisons made as the promotional activities develop. Field research such as this can be expensive, but after the initial development of questionnaires, some field research could be conducted by students to reduce costs and provide a useful work experience for marketing students.

It is essential to develop a timetable to look at the results of the market research and how they should be implemented. The main aspects which need researching are:

▦ Gauge visitor numbers at different times of the year, and as the promotional activities develop – to assess the effectiveness of the campaign.

▦ Establish how people hear about Portobello and decide to visit – to decide which promotional messages and methods are most effective.

▦ Reasons for visiting the area, and what developments they would like to see – to bring about product developments which enhance the attraction of the area to potential new and repeat visitors.

▩ Information about the profile of visitors to Portobello – age, country/area of origin, education, interests, etc – to decide which markets to target.

Target markets

It will be necessary to target two main types of visitor – Londoners and visitors to London (particularly from overseas). Londoners are relatively easy to target but are not as high spending as some visitors from overseas.

Londoners

The Londoners to be targeted will be relatively young (aged 18–40), who enjoy shopping and entertaining, discovering new areas and will have high disposable income. They will generally be 'innovators' rather than 'followers' – people who enjoy diversity and who are looking for new experiences.

Some of these will have an awareness of Portobello (it may be necessary to counteract the reputation as a drug centre, although this is not as strong as might be expected) but are likely to be less aware of everything that the area has to offer. Promotions to Londoners should stress the 'hot mix' of styles, cultures and facilities, the diversity which Portobello offers, and value for money.

Visitors to London

The prime visitor market for Portobello will be from overseas, and particularly Americans, Europeans and young Japanese people. As with Londoners, the types of people to target are those who enjoy diversity, are relatively young, and have high disposable income. They are more likely to be repeat visitors to London, rather than first-time visitors.

Many of the overseas visitors will have already heard about the market, although few of them seem to realise when it takes place and what it sells. It will be important to stress the diversity of the area as a whole, inform overseas visitors about the best times to come, and stress the 'quirkiness' of the area. Most of this type of overseas visitor are looking for what they regard as English eccentricity.

Both the Londoners and visitors to London will need to be reached through intermediaries:

- Londoners will be reached more directly, but still using life-style and London publications, and via special interest groups.

- Overseas visitors will be reached via 'influencers' such as guide books, tourist information centres, tour operators, London Tourist Board and British Tourist Authority promotion, and the media. Overseas visitors will also be reached once they are in London.

The greatest need is to inform each of these markets and make them more aware of the facilities which Portobello offers them.

Marketing tools

Marketing tools have been determined based on:

- the level of awareness of the Portobello area in the target markets;

- activities undertaken by competitors;

- the diversity and complexity of the product on offer.

The main requirements are to provide persuasive information about the Portobello area, raising awareness of facilities so that more people can be encouraged to visit.

A new 'identity' has been developed for the Portobello area, using a wordmark and 'swirl' as the logo which is to be used on promotional literature, letterheads, in advertisements and on street signage. It has been designed to appeal to a variety of markets, and through the swirl and wordmark implies movement, diversity and a slight quirkiness.

Por*to*bello

Designed by Phil Underwood, Positive Design Works

Marketing tools to be used will include the following eight items:

Promotional leaflet

A promotional leaflet will be developed, which will use persuasive copy and design to inform potential visitors about the various aspects of Portobello to encourage them to visit. It will be designed to be read before coming to the area – acting as an incentive to do so – and to be used by people once they are in the area.

It will have six two-sided panels (effectively two A4 sheets laid short end to end), folding down to $^1/_3$ A4 size to fit most standard leaflet display racks. The leaflet will cover:

▓ Portobello past – a brief history

▓ Portobello present – information about some of the main reasons for visiting Portobello:

> ▓ the music scene;
> ▓ fashion;
> ▓ food and drink;
> ▓ antiques.

▓ Best times to visit – the antiques market is only there on Saturdays so the leaflet needs to describe the various stalls and the changing atmosphere on different days of the week.

The reverse six panels include information on how to get to Portobello, as well as a map, which has descriptive information around the sides, and merging into the map about the various stalls, shops, bars, etc which can be found in the area. Around a dozen red spots scattered at different locations on the map indicate 'star discoveries' which are either particularly quirky architectural sights, excellent bars, cafes and restaurants or unusual and interesting shops. The leaflet does not explain which of these each spot is, but encourages the potential visitor to use the leaflet and walk around the area to discover these places for themselves.

Careful thought has been put into the distribution of the leaflet. It will be distributed through:

▒ the Market Office in Portobello and a temporary information stall in the antiques section;

▒ through London tourist information centres;

▒ in response to enquiries from overseas visitors;

▒ via hotels and other visitor-related outlets which border on the Portobello area.

Using these outlets will make it possible to reach visitors to London, as well as some Londoners.

It is also likely that enlargements of the map side of the leaflet will be used on street hoardings and sign-posts and at the three underground stations in the area.

Public relations activities

PR activities will be important in the promotion of Portobello. An extensive media list will need to be developed so that Londoners and the domestic market can be targeted through area-specific or special interest press/editors. The media list will cover these categories:

▒ arts and design;

▒ antiques

▒ interior design;

▒ homes/design;

▒ food;

- ▓ locals/London;

- ▓ style – men;

- ▓ style – women;

- ▓ teen;

- ▓ tourist;

- ▓ general women's;

- ▓ youth/young culture;

- ▓ lifestyle publications;

- ▓ national dailies and Sunday supplements – editors classified by interest, eg shopping.

A PR plan will be developed to ensure the targeting of this press list with a variety of press releases and features suggestions. These could be general ideas such as a feature on Christmas shopping; places to shop for Valentine's Day gifts; places to take a loved one for dinner; or more specific features looking in more detail at particular aspects of Portobello such as the growth of high-quality restaurants.

Another important element of PR activities will be liaision with the press offices at the London Tourist Board and BTA to ensure inclusion in their media activity and to arrange to host journalists and other key contacts when they are in London.

Advertising

As the marketing budget is relatively low and awareness of the area is limited, only minimal advertising will be undertaken, mainly in key visitor guides.

Direct mail

Personalised direct mail letters will be sent to key 'influencers' about Portobello – to ensure they have relevant and accurate information with which to influence potential visitors. Material will be adapted to suit the recipient. These 'influencers' will include:

▨ guide book editors throughout the world whose guides cover London;

▨ BTA offices worldwide – who advise and inform potential visitors and gather material for various publications about Britain;

▨ incoming tour operators and other organisations who make arrangements on behalf of visitors to Britain;

▨ blue badge guides who need to receive relevant material for inclusion in their commentaries and to suggest interesting places to visit to their clients.

Internet

There are already several web sites which feature the Portobello area or market. Rather than develop a new site, existing site developers will be contacted to ensure that their site contains relevant and accurate information.

London Tourist Board

Promotions will be developed in conjunction with the London Tourist Board, taking advantage of specific campaigns such as their shopping initiative.

Joint promotions

Ideas for joint promotions will be investigated as the marketing initiative develops. For example, this could include working with other markets or specialist shopping areas in London to raise awareness of London as an interesting place to shop, targeting overseas visitors. This type of promotion would have a greater impact and be more cost-effective than one which only includes Portobello.

Use of outside agencies

North Kensington City Challenge Company has limited resources in terms of staff and their time so a marketing consultant will be retained for an initial period of six months to develop and implement marketing activities, reporting to a Steering Group each month and following specific project objectives.

Monitoring

A programme of market research should be developed, using field researchers to conduct face-to-face interviews at a variety of locations on different days of the week. These interviews should be repeated every three months to assess the impact of promotional activities. Additional information should be gathered, by using anecdotal evidence and information from local market traders, restaurants and shops. Towards the end of the first year of promotional activity, this research material should then be analysed to review marketing activities and to plan for the following year.

3

PROMOTIONAL TOOLS

INTRODUCTION

Marketing promotion is essentially the process of communicating with selected target markets. Most promotional activities require an investment of time and money which can reap excellent rewards if they are carefully planned and executed.

The 'menu' of promotional activities is diverse and includes:

- promotional print;
- public relations (PR);
- advertising;
- the Internet;
- direct mail;
- sales activities;
- exhibition attendance;
- joint promotions with other organisations.

SELECTING PROMOTIONAL TOOLS

The following chapters offer guidance on each of these activities, but first of all you will need to select the most appropriate methods for you.

The promotional tools you select will essentially be determined by your target markets and marketing budget. On the subject of budgets, it is worth mentioning that few organisations consider their marketing budget to be big enough. It is not unusual for small budgets to be blamed for a lack of success. A bigger budget can make life easier but it is possible to make an impact without major expense.

The case study about Discover Islington in Section Four demonstrates how carefully targeted activities do not have to be expensive. Indeed, small budgets can mean marketing efforts are more focused and carefully planned.

Just as you have hopefully spent some time thinking about your marketing plan, it is important to set timescales and plan promotional activities carefully. Whenever possible you should test promotional ideas before launching them to the wider world, and make sure that you build in monitoring methods.

A blanket approach will not be as successful as one which pays careful consideration to each market segment and its needs. Some of the factors which should influence your choice of promotional tools are: target markets, the product, competition and product awareness.

Target markets

What promotional methods are they used to? Is it better to use the ones which they accept and which experience proves they react to, or perhaps make an impact by trying something different?

Consumer and trade marketing are very different. Consumers need to be given information and messages to make them want to buy, possibly through the travel trade. In this sense consumer marketing is the 'pull' – encouraging consumers to demand the product through appropriate distribution channels.

The travel trade need to be given information which inspires them to sell the product to consumers. This is a 'push' campaign. Messages designed for consumers will not always have a positive impact on the travel trade. For the travel trade magic words like 'commission' or 'profit' are more likely to work than 'relax and enjoy...'.

The product

Some products are quite complex, ie those that might need personal explanation, so some promotional methods will be unsuitable. It is very difficult to convey atmosphere or ambiance through some media so promotional tools need to be adapted accordingly.

Competition

Some activities will be determined by those of your competitors so you should always try to be aware of what they are planning. If they undertake a major advertising campaign and your operation looks like it could lose market share, the only option may be to retaliate with a stronger campaign (but not necessarily more expensive) or you may decide to focus on different markets for more impact.

Product awareness

New products which are just being launched generally need more promotion than established ones – advertising and PR activities are likely to reach a larger number of potential customers than personal sales. Conversely old products which are perhaps becoming stale will also need an extra push from time to time.

Working on the principle that all purchasers move through the five stages of: unawareness; awareness; understanding; conviction and response it is necessary to consider which point they have reached and choose promotional tools according to their level of awareness.

The following uses the example of the area of Fife in Scotland. Let us assume that the tourism officer there wishes to increase the numbers of higher spending, longer staying visitors from overseas.

The tourism officer first of all needs to identify potential market segments and determine their level of awareness of the destination.

Unawareness

It is difficult to be precise about the profiles of visitors at the unawareness stage. Little information is known about the market beyond a general category of people who do not currently come to Fife in any sizable numbers, and who might be referred to under the geographic description of 'Rest of the World'.

At this stage the potential visitors will not only have never heard of Fife but their geographic knowledge of Britain in general is likely to be hazy. It is more appropriate for the BTA to undertake a PR and advertising campaign on behalf of Britain as a whole, than for the Fife tourism officer to try to educate these visitors. *Promotional tools*: advertising and PR campaign; *message*: general.

Awareness

In the awareness stage countries and segments can be identified more precisely, and promotions undertaken by the BTA or Scottish Tourist Board. Potential visitors have to be moved on from the awareness to the understanding stage before the Fife tourism officer can become fully involved in promotional activities. *Promotional tools*: advertising, PR and some general publications; *message*: general information with more detail than earlier stage.

Understanding

At the understanding stage it becomes possible to identify and research segments of potential visitors and to identify particular strategies to target them. The Scottish Tourist Board would be involved at this level, with some input from the area tourist board in Fife. *Promotional tools*: advertising, PR, exhibitions and publications; *message*: information becomes more detailed, focused and persuasive.

Conviction

By the conviction stage the segments become clearer and can be easily identified. Promotion and information dissemination is carried out by the area tourist board, tour operators and accommodation providers. *Promotional tools*: advertising, PR, exhibitions, publications, direct marketing and personal contact; *message*: more focused and persuasive, with detailed information on specific tour operators, accommodation listings, attractions, etc.

Response

The response stage means that visitors can actually be identified and possibly even named. Promotion can now be undertaken at a more local level, including district tourism officers and visitor attractions. *Promotional tools*: similar to Conviction stage but with much more focused messages; *message*: highly focused and specific, action-oriented and capable of directing visitors to particular attractions or routes.

CHOOSING PROMOTIONAL MESSAGES

After selecting promotional tools to suit your target markets and product, promotional messages will need to be adapted.

Most promotional activities work through the 'AIDA principle', which stands for *Attention*, *Interest*, *Desire* and *Action*.

To be effective your brochure will need to:

▒ grab *attention*;

▒ appeal to the readers' self-*interest*;

▒ arouse the *desire* to buy;

▒ urge the reader to take *action*.

For brochure producers this means that the promotional message will depend on several key factors:

▒ The target market.

▒ Channel of distribution – for example, different messages may be necessary for tour operators, members of the public and tourist information centres.

▦ The type of response you need to evoke – these usually divide into rational and emotional appeals.

▦ Promotional method – for example, you need a stronger and shorter message for radio advertisements than you do for a direct sales campaign when a salesperson can explain in more detail.

You should always be aware of the reasons why people buy specific products. These will vary with different products, circumstances and sets of people. Sometimes people appear to be buying for reasons different to their real motivations. By understanding the reasons people buy you are more likely to be able to appeal to them.

These are some of the key reasons why we buy particular products:

▦ *Price* – It may be that something appears to offer value for money. Sometimes we buy more expensive products because we believe they will be better than cheaper ones or we like the image they convey.

▦ *Health* – Holidays are seen as healthy activities, offering the chance to relax. We buy some products because we think they are good for us.

▦ *Social* – This may be a chance to be together with friends or family, or simply a desire not to get left out. Some products are purchased because it becomes normal to have them, rather than for rational reasons.

▦ *Status* – Some products offer a chance to impress. Others are bought because they make a statement about the purchaser or make the purchaser feel good about themselves.

BROCHURES AND PRINT MATERIAL

Brochures demonstrate the benefits which an organisation has to offer. Many tourism products are not tangible. By describing them in print, brochures become the only 'evidence' of the product so it is important that the feel and quality of the experience are conveyed by the brochure. Destinations and tours are particularly difficult to promote without print material which explains what is on offer.

Before you begin to write and design any brochures you will need to step back and consider these key points:

Why do you need a brochure – what is it for?

For example, it could be to:

▓ inform people about your facilities;

▓ encourage them to make a booking;

▓ encourage them to stay longer in your area or hotel.

In many cases it will be for a combination of purposes – ensure you jot these down as part of your brochure brief. Consider also where the brochure will be used. Pre- and post-arrival print fulfil differing needs.

Who will be your main target markets?

By now it should be clear that all promotions need targets and you need to set these down before undertaking promotional activities. When writing and designing brochures you will be more successful if you paint a picture of a key reader in your mind. It is easier to write better copy by imagining you are speaking to one typical reader. Ask yourself:

▓ What are their ages?

▓ What are their interests?

▓ Where do they come from?

▓ Are they likely to be direct consumers or intermediaries such as travel agents or tour operators?

▓ Are they potential new clients or existing clients?

▦ Do you need to persuade them to switch from another product or just that yours is a good one?

How will your brochures be distributed?

Your brochure will only evoke a positive response if it reaches your target markets. Good design, photography and copywriting will help you to do this. Distribution is also critical.

This is a key issue and needs to be thought through, if only because distribution is expensive and you need to be certain you have allowed a sufficient budget to cover it. As a rough guide, once you have worked out the cost of design and print, you should allow as much as one third again for distribution costs.

Many brochures are binned, not just by their recipients, but by the people who produce them, because they have overestimated the number they need or because the information in the brochure is not accurate.

Distribution methods will have an impact on the number you need to produce as well as the preferred format for the leaflet. If it is to be distributed through standard brochure racks the most popular finished size is one-third A4, with the name of your establishment towards the top of the leaflet. Using a standard format and usual distribution methods such as this will probably mean you need more brochures. If you decide on a more unusual format like a square brochure which is to be mailed, the print run will depend more on the size of your mailing list.

Consider how many brochures you will distribute:

▦ By direct mail – is your mailing list up to date?

▦ At exhibitions – which ones?

▦ Through brochure racks – where and how?

▦ Through tourist information centres – which ones? Have you checked that they want your brochures?

▦ Through *ad hoc* outlets such as libraries and community centres – how will you get them there? Have you checked that they will display them?

░ Through BTA overseas offices – do not just send a batch of leaflets (they will almost certainly be rejected). Find out if the office will take them and at what charge.

If you are not sure how many brochures to produce, do a quick calculation of the number of people on your mailing list, and call some of the outlets through which you plan to distribute them. Ask for their advice. They will probably welcome being asked – visitor information centres are often frustrated by the unsolicited bulk supplies of irrelevant literature which they receive.

The main brochure distribution services are able to give quite accurate estimates of the numbers of brochures they can distribute on your behalf. If you are uncertain how you are going to distribute bulk supplies of brochures, it is usually worth speaking to your local tourist board, who may also have special rates for members through a brochure distribution company.

Making your brochure work

Remember the AIDA principle and think about each of the four stages and how they relate to brochures.

Attention

░ Catch the reader's attention and get them to pick up the brochure.

░ Make the reader open the first page.

░ Make the reader keep reading the brochure until all the information is absorbed.

Interest

░ The brochure must look interesting to the reader.

░ The brochure must *be* interesting to the reader (to keep their attention).

░ The brochure should be easy to read and understand.

Desire

▓ You will need to make sure the reader distinguishes your product from others.

▓ The brochure should demonstrate why your product is good.

▓ The brochure should persuade the reader to agree that it is the only one for them.

Action

▓ It should be easy to take action and easy to make a booking or buy.

Planning the brochure or print material

Collect examples of competitors' brochures and samples of print material you think work well so you can adapt some of the best ideas when you start to develop your own. Before you start writing copy or briefing a designer, make sure you consider the answers to these questions:

▓ What sort of people are the main targets for the brochure?

▓ What level of awareness and understanding of your product do they have?

▓ Will the distribution methods for the brochure affect the content in any way?

▓ What is the main message you want to convey? Try to identify one key message which you want your brochure to give.

▓ What are the main benefits which you wish to stress? What do they mean for the reader?

Copywriting

Of all aspects of brochure production, copywriting can be the most difficult, and yet it is often given little thought. Vast sums of money are spent on upgrading the quality of print and design. They are both important but what about the words you use? Most organisations could make a major improvement to their brochures without spending a penny – just by thinking more carefully about the copy. By following a few simple rules you can vastly improve most print material.

What do people want to read? You will be able to write more persuasive and direct copy if you picture one typical reader in your mind. This will help you write as if you were speaking to them. What are they wearing? What sort of words and ideas will they react to?

Jot down some of the words you think that reader might like to read. For example, parents will warm to words like 'fun', 'educational' and 'safe'. Busy couples looking for a weekend away are more likely to react to 'romantic' and 'relaxing'.

Try to identify one key message which you want your brochure to give. For example, it might convey an overall feeling of quality, or portray a sense of serenity and relaxation, or stress value for money.

Make a note of the benefits you want to sell. Think why your typical reader might buy your product or experience. We are all motivated by different things, depending on our social background and personal needs.

Many products are sold in ways which do not bear a direct relation to the product itself. Watch television and you will see that emotional selling works particularly well. Perfume manufacturers do not sell smell – they promise romance. Car advertisers do not promote a means of transport – they offer excitement or a macho image.

Before you begin writing, jot down the points you want to cover as they occur to you, then sort them into a logical order.

You!

You will grab your readers' attention by addressing them directly. The word 'you' instantly grabs attention. Readers identify with it and instinctively assume it means them.

Many brochures describe 'our facilities' which isolates the reader and focuses on features instead of benefits. Sentences should be turned round to make them more appealing. For example:

> All our bedrooms are individually designed and have
> en-suite facilities

should become:

> You'll be able to relax in one of our individually designed
> bedrooms with a private bathroom.

The second sentence is immediately more appealing. Using questions also helps to involve and persuade the reader, particularly if the answer is almost certainly 'Yes'. For example:

> Wouldn't you just love to escape the pressures of
> everyday life and relax in the countryside? Hotel Snooze
> offers the perfect get-away break.

The *benefits* of what you have to offer are the real reason why people will buy. If your prospective guest were to read, 'You'll feel relaxed and refreshed, enjoying the fresh air and tranquillity at Hotel Snooze', they would be even more likely to make a booking. But remember, you must write something which sounds credible and appeals to your target audience.

Some copywriting hints

▓ Headlines are useful for attracting attention. Responses will be more positive if you: make a promise (which you can fulfil); offer the solution to a problem; describe a good strong benefit.

▓ Link headlines to the first sentence of your body copy so readers are enticed to read further.

▓ It is worth starting with something newsworthy or different, a surprising fact rather than a standard introduction.

▓ Use specifics, not generalisations: 'adventure playground, muddling maze and glorious gardens' works better than 'something for everyone'.

▒ Short everyday words, short sentences and short paragraphs are easier to read. Short sentences have impact.

▒ Demonstrate the benefits of what you have to offer in the main copy.

▒ Do not exaggerate – we have all become used to words like 'amazing', 'incredible' and 'fantastic offer'. Your copy will be more credible if you give real examples, and show what you mean by good use of illustrations.

▒ Use trigger words. We have become accustomed to seeing many of these but for some reason we still react to them. Useful trigger words include: free, new, guarantee, opportunity, service, save, love and extra.

▒ People like stories. Anecdotes and intrigue are more likely to attract than bland descriptions.

Designing your brochure

Desktop publishing packages have made it possible for all of us to become designers, but few of us will ever have the talent to do so. DIY design looks like DIY design. Professional designers cost money – because they are worth it.

When choosing a designer, try to find someone with whom you will enjoy working. Design should be part of a creative process and you need to be able to express yourself clearly. It helps if you have set your budget and any restrictions before you start speaking to designers and printers.

Ask to see examples of the designer's work to make sure they are capable of producing brochures suitable for your target markets. Some designers specialise in particular types of work. It is not always the best policy to go to a designer who specialises in your area of the tourism industry. A designer who has not worked for your type of organisation before may bring a fresher approach.

Give your designer as much background information as possible about your aims and organisation – anything is useful because it helps them get a 'feel' for the way you wish to present your product. Remember to tell the designer about any house-styles which already exist and which you want to keep. Provide bromides or disks with logos and any other material which you need to use.

If you have collected examples of other brochures which you think work particularly well it is useful to show them to your designer. It is equally good to show them examples of things which you do not like so they can visibly gauge what you are looking for.

Set a schedule for work to be undertaken and bear in mind that producing a brochure can be a long process. Designers and printers can obviously work to much tighter deadlines but an ideal timetable would be:

Week 1	brief designer
Week 3	meet to look at roughs and ideas, leaving the designer to develop one idea to full visuals
Week 4	visual produced, including colour swatches and using actual copy – this is effectively the first proof stage and the point after which corrections begin to incur costs
Week 5	return corrections to designer and sign off the final proof
Week 6	marked-up artwork to the printer
Week 7	final proofs from the printer
Week 8–9	receive brochures – print time will depend on quantity to be produced, number of colours and type of finishing

Design timetables and methods are developing rapidly with increased use of computer packages and the ability to send artwork 'down the line' to printers rather than posting pasted up artwork.

General design hints

▓ When asking for a design quote, ask for an all-inclusive price so you can budget accurately. Some design quotations exclude artwork or additional expenses – make sure you know what these might be.

▓ Common sense can make a dramatic difference to design success. For example, brochures for display racks should always have the title wording at the top so it is not obscured by other brochures. If your brochure includes a tear off slip for further information, try completing it yourself to make sure the spaces are large enough for legible hand-writing.

▓ Get your designer to show you the exact pantones they plan to use. These are similar to paint sample cards, showing each colour and their pantone reference number. Consider whether the brochure will be legible in the chosen colours.

▓ Don't sacrifice clarity and readability for the sake of 'interesting design'. It is easier to read text in dark colours than light ones. Beware of choosing colours and a style which you like, rather than ones which appeal to your target reader.

▓ When checking artwork and proofs, make sure that pictures are in the right place and the right way round.

▓ Check type matter carefully and watch out for simple spelling errors. By the time you give your copy to the designer, it should be as word-perfect as possible. Author's corrections made at proof stage will be charged for and can become expensive.

▓ Double check that all information is correct and descriptions fair and accurate. Ensure that you have permission to use any borrowed photographs or illustrations.

▓ Keep your original artwork in case you need it use it again, which will avoid new reproduction costs.

Photography

Most brochures include at least some photographs, and nearly all brochures could be improved by investing in good professional photography. If you are using a professional photographer, decide in advance what you will need to photograph and ensure everything is prepared before the photographer arrives. Do not be afraid of asking if you can look through the camera lens to see if particular photographs will include the things you need to show.

Good colour transparencies are the best format for use in brochures. The better the original the better the result. Bad quality photographs are rarely improved by the print process. Make sure that you caption each picture. A caption is more eye-catching than a label. For example, a bedroom is obviously a bedroom and does not need labelling as such, but a caption along the lines of 'treat yourself to a rest' is more compelling.

Consider the content of each photograph you use and try to avoid anything which will date them such as very fashionable clothes. It helps if you can show people having fun or carrying out appropriate activities. Make sure the people you use look like your target markets. There is little point showing a family with young children if you do not want to attract children.

Try to avoid obvious photographs which do little to sell your product. Hotels often feature a photograph of the receptionist grinning as she lifts a phone – there are other aspects of hotels which are more likely to sell. Some buildings are difficult to photograph or do not look appealing. If this is the case for you consider using photographs of other aspects or nearby areas if they are appropriate.

When sending photographs to the designer or printer make sure you pack them adequately and avoid using any staples or paperclips which may damage them. Always have copies made of good photographs and transparencies in case the originals get lost or damaged. When budgeting for professional photography bear in mind that you could use the photographs for other purposes such as advertisements or PR activities so professional photography may be better value for money than it first appears.

Working with printers

Print techniques are constantly changing and printers seem particularly adept at developing jargon which lay people cannot understand. It is often worthwhile asking your designer to manage the whole process for you. They will usually be able to negotiate good rates with printers and ensure that the final print looks exactly how they designed it to look. Designers also understand the print process and are less likely to be confused by the amazing array of printers' terms.

Obtaining print quotes

This should not prevent you from obtaining comparative quotes from other printers, and then asking your designer to work directly with whichever printer you choose. Beware of choosing the cheapest printer you can find. You will probably find significant differences in cost but the very cheapest is unlikely to be the best. Whatever price you are quoted, you will probably need to add 10 per cent on to the price, to take account of any changes and unexpected problems. There is nearly always some unexpected change or cost.

Use the following as a checklist of essential information for your printer when asking for a quote:

▓ Quantity required (most people also ask for a 'run-on' quote per 1000 or 10,000).

▓ Size of finished brochure, and type/weight of paper to be used. Will the cover require a different weight paper? Most printers will provide samples.

▓ Number of colours.

▓ Printed on one or both sides? How many pages?

▓ Are proofs required?

▓ How the origination material will be provided (ask your designer) – disk type, number of artworks, pictures, illustrations, transparencies, etc.

▓ Any additional requirements such as folding and finishing.

▓ Deadline for final delivery.

Size

When deciding on the format and size of print material, ensure it is appropriate for your purposes, and easy to distribute, ie so that it fits brochure display stands or standard envelopes. Unusual size leaflets (such as square ones) grab attention but are expensive to produce and distribute. The paper has to be specially cut and cannot be sent out in standard-sized envelopes. A standard size leaflet such as A4 folded down to one third A4 (gatefold) is easiest to use as it fits into standard brochure racks and envelopes.

Quantity

The most expensive part of printing is preparation. It is cheaper to print extra copies on a long run than to order a reprint. Bear in mind that additional copies cost very little to print, but distribution costs may prevent their use. Another consideration may be storage because boxes of leaflets are heavy and cumbersome. Do you have adequate storage space for the print run you want to order?

Paper

The weight of the paper (or as most would think of it, the thickness) depends on the size of the print item and if it is to be used in mailings, you will need to consider postal rates. Lighter paper is slightly cheaper but the quality of print material can suffer because the colour can 'bleed' through the thin pages.

Remember that print quotes must be in writing for them to be binding. Beware of asking for a print quote and assuming it will still be valid if you do not use the printer for a few weeks or months. Paper prices vary enormously and could easily increase if you do not use the printer shortly after receiving the quotation. Paper prices can account for as much as 50 per cent of the total print price.

Colour

Two-colour print can be very attractive, but it does not have the impact and selling power of full-colour. If full-colour is too expensive, check whether the printer can meet your budget with a combination of full-colour one side and two-colour on the reverse. Alternatively you could use two colours with their tones to give a wider range.

Finishing

This stage covers folding, trimming and stitching, or stapling, for which an additional charge is usually made. Print material needs time to dry before it is folded. If you press the printer to deliver too quickly you may find that the colour bleeds on to other copies or pages because it has not had time to dry.

Some general tips

▓ You have already identified your typical reader so write to that person in ordinary everyday English. Read what you have written aloud to check if it sounds stilted. Write as if you are talking to someone; and try to avoid pompous language or jargon.

▓ Do not try to crowd your brochure with words and explanations. The best copy is often the shortest. If you have a strong product which photographs well, let pictures tell the story, with the minimum number of words.

▓ Try to avoid using long passages of text. If you need to do so, break up the text by using cross-headings – words or phrases picked out of the text and highlighted.

▓ Before you send your brochure off to the printers, show the mock-up version to people within your target markets and ask for their comments. You may find that things which seem obvious to you are not to other people, particularly if you have used jargon.

▓ Do not forget to include a map in your brochure to show how accessible your venue or area is. It can be useful to mention other landmarks or major cities and describe how far they are in travelling time rather than distance so people relate more easily to the location.

▓ Make sure your copy is readable, especially if older people or children are likely to read it. Unusual typefaces might attract attention but they are distracting and difficult to read.

▧ Tell the truth! Do not oversell so that people are disappointed, but do remember that you can often minimalise negatives by making them into a feature. It is amazing how slanting floors and rickety old furniture can suddenly become quaint signs of an ancient building, not one which is falling apart.

▧ Your brochure's main purpose will probably be to sell. If it is, you must also make it easy to buy. Ensure that your contact details such as address, telephone, fax and e-mail numbers are prominently displayed. People often feel more comfortable if they have a contact name as well. You can avoid the problem of printing names of staff who may leave, and monitor the success of your brochure by including a fictitious name on the brochure. Do not forget to inform all staff about the booking name!

PUBLIC RELATIONS

Public relations (PR) activities are about directing carefully selected messages to key target groups. They can range from ensuring that all your staff present a tidy and friendly image to the public, to lobbying Members of Parliament and trying to obtain coverage in the media.

Effective PR can influence a vast range of different groups of people, encouraging them to buy your product. However, you will have little control over whether or not your efforts are successful because you are not paying for coverage or people's opinions.

PR activities might include:

▧ Lobbying politicians and opinion formers to improve services or legislate on matters which are important to you. For example, regional tourist boards might lobby for improved access to their area, or to encourage acceptance of an airport development.

▧ Convincing opinion formers in your local community to support your activities and encourage others to do so, often through positive word-of-mouth publicity.

▓ Initiating positive media coverage of your activities through selected media by issuing press releases or invitations to members of the media to experience your facilities first-hand.

▓ Developing contacts with local, national and specialist media and being ready to help them should they call with any requests for information or interviews on a subject related to your activities, thus developing a reputation as a spokesperson in your field.

Improving public relations

PR is essentially about developing and maintaining awareness of your product, so that people are encouraged to buy it. You can influence and attract your target markets by carrying out PR activities which generally show your organisation in a favourable light.

These activities may not show tangible results but should be part of developing a successful business. Networking is a common way of getting business, developing word-of-mouth referrals and personal contacts.

Some of these activities do not relate directly to your target markets, but will help to raise your profile. It is worth making time to:

▓ hold open days and invite the press, members of the public or travel trade to see the facilities which you offer in an informal setting;

▓ develop links with other people involved in the tourism industry or similar field as you. This might be a trade body or membership of your local tourist board;

▓ speak at conferences, lecture or write articles on your specialist subject for consumer or trade press;

▓ attend exhibitions and events where you will have the opportunity to meet the press or buyers such as tour operators.

PR activities

The bulk of PR activities centre around channels of communication such as the press, and broadcast media. This section concentrates on these.

Advantages of PR

▓ Most PR activities are low cost and rely more on resourcefulness than resources, unlike advertising.

▓ When carried out effectively, PR activities can reach a very wide audience, helping to raise your profile and position your product in a positive light.

▓ PR activities can help to inform the public and generate sales during quiet or off-peak periods.

▓ PR activities can result in media coverage which is viewed much more positively than advertising. Coverage is often perceived as an endorsement of your product.

▓ Information which is published as a result of PR activities appears impartial whereas advertising is often treated with suspicion.

▓ PR activities can be carefully targeted, to appeal to specific and even specialist, markets.

Disadvantages of PR

▓ Unlike advertising you cannot control the result of PR activities. As many as 90 per cent of all press releases are simply thrown in the bin.

▓ Sending out press releases can be time-consuming. Forward planning is essential so you must have a sustained and positive approach. Occasional PR activities are unlikely to have an impact.

▓ You are unlikely to know whether your press release has been used by all the media you have sent it to. When they receive your release most editors will make a decision whether to publish or not, without contacting you.

▦ Press releases are rarely published in their entirety. Most of the time, the first paragraphs are the main ones to be repro-duced. This might mean that information is misinterpreted.

Planning PR activities

Whatever PR activities you undertake, you should plan them in advance. Consider your target markets, and identify key mes-sages which you wish to communicate to them. You might wish to:

▦ convey a general image or feeling, such as building an image as a caring company, or offering value for money or diversity;

▦ promote a particular range of events or packages;

▦ develop off-peak business;

▦ target new markets who have a low level of awareness of your product, and who require more detailed information about the 'experience' you can offer them.

The next, and most important step is to draw up a timetable of activities. Good timing is critical to the success of many PR activities. Your timetable should take into consideration the times when people make decisions to book or come to your area, and highlight any times when you will be looking for extra business, as well as including any special events, whether they are internal or external.

Use a calendar to ensure you do not miss key dates when people might be persuaded to buy your product. For example, bank holidays and special events like Mother's Day. For each of the featured dates you will need to work out which publication or programme dates might be relevant, and when they need information from you.

For example, if you are arranging an Easter Sunday Egg Treas-ure Hunt and Easter falls in the middle of April you might decide that your target market is local families with young children and that some of the local press could be interested in the event.

Some people might decide to take part after having read about the event in the Sunday paper, but most of them will have planned their Easter Sunday in advance.

This will probably mean that you want to be featured in the midweek editions of local daily newspapers and in the previous week's edition of the weekly paper. Monthly magazines often bear one date and appear a month earlier so if your area has a monthly magazine you will probably want to appear in the March rather than the April edition.

There is no guarantee that any of these publications will publish details of your event, unless you take out paid advertising. However, you can significantly increase your chances simply by sending information at appropriate times.

Bear in mind lead times, which may be a month in advance for weekly publications and up to three or four months in advance for monthly publications. That means that the March edition of the magazine you wish to be featured in could well be planned before Christmas. You will need to take all these factors into consideration in your PR timetable and list the media you plan to approach and different types of story for each date.

If you wish to target daily papers, remember that papers particularly welcome information which reaches them on Monday morning, when other news is thin on the ground. They are also more likely to publish information in July and August when political news items are less frequent.

It is useful to produce general information sheets about your organisation so you have some basic facts readily at hand. These can be included with press releases as background information. They should be brief and to the point, including information about key personnel, facilities, and advance notice of any special events.

Choosing suitable media

Identify the programmes your target markets watch and media they are likely to read and develop a contact list. There are several professional directories available which give details of media contacts for trade and consumer press or broadcast media. They can appear quite expensive but save a lot of work, particularly if you need to target specialist media which might be difficult to find.

PiMS publish an excellent range of media directories with up-to-date contact details for different types of press and broadcast media in the UK and overseas. You can obtain these from:

PiMS UK Ltd
PiMS House
Mildmay Avenue
London
N1 4RS
Telephone: 0171 226 1000
Fax: 0171 704 1360

It is a good idea to at least see programmes or glance through copies of the publications on your media, to ensure you are sending out appropriate information. If you have asked for a media pack to consider advertising in any of those publications you should have already received a sample copy as well as a features list, which might give you ideas for future activities.

Writing press releases

There are accepted rules for writing press releases which it is useful to follow. Of course there are times when you will make a bigger impact by using alternative methods or creating a splash through less orthodox practices but if you are just beginning to use PR it might be safer to follow the rules. Journalists are not afraid of ridiculing PR activities which go wrong!

General notes on the format of press releases

▓ Do not use complicated language but try to write in a similar tone to the publications or media you are targeting. Your press release will stand a better chance of being used if the journalist's work is minimal. If you use an appropriate style this will help.

▓ Try to limit your press release to one side of A4, preferably typed using double spacing and wide margins so the copy is easy for journalists to edit.

▓ Make it clear that your press release is a press release – say so on the letterhead.

▓ Use a short and punchy headline to grab attention, avoiding jargon and making it really sound like news.

▓ Make the point of the story clear in the first paragraph. Try to encompass the essence of the story in the first sentence to entice the reader to continue reading.

▓ Be factual and objective. The release should be informative and not read like 'hard-sell' full of PR puff.

▓ The release should be written in the third person, without using 'I' or 'we'.

▓ Remember that most press releases are edited 'bottom up'. This means that the last part of the release is the most likely to be chopped, so do not put important information there – it should be in the first paragraph.

▓ Make sure that you have included all relevant details like the time, date, venue and description of an event.

▓ Include the date of the release at the foot of the page.

▓ Remember that your press release is supposed to stimulate editors into wanting to write about or feature your product. To do this, it must be newsworthy, interesting and stimulating.

▓ Make it easy for the journalist to react by putting your contact name, address and telephone/fax numbers at the end of the release. If you have any additional important information such as opening times, add those at the end under a general note. If there is a large amount of relevant detail, attach it as an appendix.

▓ A good tip is to read through the information you have written. If a likely reaction to the release could be 'So what?' you will need to either re-write the story or consider another angle.

Storylines

There are basically two types of press release: *news* and *features*. There are several other angles which you could use:

Surveys

Details of surveys and reports are often published, usually stating their origin. These are not always official statistics – light-hearted versions are also welcome.

Be an authority

Editors like to have people to whom they can refer and quote when talking about certain issues. You can raise your profile by telephoning editors or sending your comments on relevant issues or even offering articles. If you wish to become known as an authority, it also helps if you are a spokesperson on behalf of a trade organisation or local group.

You will often have better chances of generating publicity if you join together with other like-minded organisations. For example, a hotel will find it quite difficult to generate publicity but is more likely to raise its profile by teaming up with a local charity, attraction or group of hotels.

Features suggestions

You can encourage editors to include information about you by suggesting articles or features to them. These might include opinions, a look behind the scenes or 'how to' articles.

Readers offers and competitions

Offers should always be carefully targeted to the programme or publication, and their target market. Making an offer or providing a competition prize will cost you money, but is often worth the publicity which it generates and you may be able to develop a mailing list as a result.

Photography

Good photographs help to make your story or press release livelier and more interesting. You might succeed in getting a newspaper photographer if you set up a photo opportunity and phone the news or picture desk in advance. However, if another more newsworthy event happens at the same time you will have missed your chance.

If you use your own photographer you will have the photographs for future use and some newspapers may still be interested in using them, even if they are not exclusives.

If you are going to create a photo opportunity think carefully about the type of picture which is most likely to attract attention in your target markets. The best photographs usually:

▦ show something about to happen;

▦ show something happening;

▦ show something has just happened.

This generally means action-oriented photographs because they make places come alive. You might have to set up the shot and it may look a little contrived. These types of photographs can still be successful if they are imaginative. Think carefully about ways of making your photographs newsworthy. If they include famous people, cute animals or children this is relatively easy. Otherwise you might need to consider an unusual angle, look behind the scenes, intriguing setting or just a good caption.

Ensure that you have plentiful copies of any photographs or transparencies because they are rarely returned, or it takes forever to get them back. Make sure you label them with your contact details.

Develop a photograph and slide library so you can produce illustrations at a moment's notice. The most useful format is 6 × 8 inches for black and white print and colour transparencies. Do not forget to caption them and provide supporting information on a separate piece of paper.

Crisis management

Not all publicity is good publicity. There are times when bad publicity could ruin your reputation. These might be natural disasters such as a flood, an outbreak of food poisoning or negative comments from the public or opinion formers.

When you are planning your PR activities it is a good idea to sit down and consider what you would do if disaster struck and you were about to receive negative publicity. By planning in case of such an eventuality you will feel more secure and be able to minimise the effects.

Consider the types of event which might result in such a situation, and draw up an outline plan to deal with them. The first task will be to agree on a single spokesperson, preferably with experience of handling the media, so that one strong message is always given out instead of conflicting and potentially confusing messages.

At regular intervals ensure that you have updated your list of home phone numbers for staff so that you can speak to the relevant people immediately in case of need. Ensure that all staff know who the spokesperson is.

Imagine each of the worst-case scenarios and draw up how you would deal with them, including looking at the company position on each event. Draw up draft statements. These may be general cover-alls which buy time, such as 'we are looking at the full details of xyz and will be making a full statement in due course'.

Overseas press

If you are trying to attract overseas visitors, developing contacts with overseas press should be an integral part of your plan. The BTA invites considerable numbers of journalists to Britain every year so they can experience facilities at first hand. If you are willing to host such visits, you should get in touch with your regional or area tourist board and directly with the BTA press office.

You should also include the BTA press office on your media list, because they sift through the releases they receive and pass them on to their contacts where relevant, so the BTA could help to generate wider coverage of your stories. Bear in mind that overseas media are probably also working to tight deadlines and will need information even more in advance than do their UK counterparts.

You are more likely to secure overseas coverage if you can join with other organisations to promote a total experience, rather than just one small aspect of Britain.

General hints to make your PR campaign more successful

▨ Set clear objectives and determine the over-riding message which you want to convey.

▨ Choose your target markets and individual segments carefully in advance and ensure that you develop appropriate media lists.

▨ Create relevant stories and press releases and follow the general rules to produce them.

▨ Introduce and follow up stories wherever possible by telephoning journalists to ask them if the press release was relevant and what kind of information they need.

ADVERTISING

Advertising allows you to promote a specific message to a wide audience – for a fee. It can be an extremely expensive promotional tool which is notoriously difficult to evaluate. Hence the frequent comment: 'I think half of my advertising is a waste of time – I just do not know which half'.

It is easy to imagine advertising as just one promotional tool, but in effect it can make use of so many different media and methods, it is almost a range of promotional tools in itself.

Advertising is good for creating and building 'awareness' but this is not necessarily the same as building sales. There are few organisations which cannot benefit in some way from an advertising campaign, but to avoid wasted effort and expense, it must be even more carefully planned than any other promotional activity.

Setting objectives

You will probably have one of two main general objectives for advertising, sometimes a combination of both:

▓ To develop a new market, and create awareness (and potentially sales) among customers who have never tried your product.

▓ To encourage previous customers to use your product or service again, or to try another aspect of it.

The nature of any advertising campaign will be determined largely by the objectives set and budgets available. Before placing advertising you need to take into consideration:

▓ the role advertising will play in your overall marketing plan;

▓ the characteristics of target markets;

▓ the type of response you are likely to achieve from target markets.

Advertising usually has either tactical or strategic objectives. *Strategic advertising* is concerned with creating an awareness of markets, and of products, of developing an organisation's identity and image. Strategic advertising takes a more long-term view.

Tactical advertising is aimed at specific market segments and persuading them to go to a particular place or buy a certain service, sometimes at a particular time. Tactical advertising takes a more short to medium-term view.

Target markets

Target markets must be clearly defined. Most advertising works best with just one key message. This is especially important if you can only afford to buy a few lines or small space. Faced with a small budget and only a couple of centimetres to fill, many organisations react by trying to get the greatest value for money. They cram the space with descriptions and detail so the overriding feeling is one of confusion or crowding.

Choosing one main message will help to give even the smallest company a stronger identity. This comes back once again to selling benefits rather than features, and stressing the Unique Selling Points. Obviously there is a need for a certain level of information as well, but even this should be presented in the right tone for the target market.

Selection of media

However much you plan your advertising in advance, there will always be occasions when an advertising salesperson telephones you with a 'special offer'. Some of these might be genuine. Most are not. You should do your best to resist – there will always be another opportunity and your advertising will be much more effective if it is proactive and planned rather than reliant on those last-minute special offers, especially if they are for new publications which no one has heard of and which disappear almost instantly.

The selection of appropriate media is usually based on three criteria.

1. *Cost of space* in the print media and time on radio, TV and cinema screen. Cost is obviously very important and is expressed in terms of cost per thousand contacts (CPT). While being a useful yardstick it only provides an estimate of potential readers or people who may see an advertisement. Usually the larger the circulation the lower is the cost per thousand. The CPT figure will also enable you to compare advertising costs with other forms of promotion, such as direct mail.
2. *Suitability* – if graphics, colour or movement are required the medium must be suitable.

3. *Appropriateness* – the chosen medium must be appropriate for the product or service being promoted and clearly targeted.

Before booking any space or time, telephone the advertising departments of the media you are interested in and ask for a copy of their media pack. This outlines the various advertising opportunities, costs, and profile of readers, viewers or listeners, as well as giving technical data for the publication or programme.

For most organisations their budgetary restrictions will limit their choice to advertising in publications rather than on television or radio. Television has been proven as an excellent and very persuasive medium but is expensive. Not only is the cost of time slots expensive but also the production of good advertisements. If you have a sufficient budget for television advertising you should use an advertising agency to help you buy the time as well as produce an effective advertisement.

Radio advertising is cheaper than television and can be useful for events and tourism products which are easy to buy such as well-known attractions. Radio advertising is less effective for products and services which need detailed explanations.

The choice of publications in which to advertise is vast. In addition to local and national press, there are also special interest magazines and tourist board guides. If you run any special interest holidays or even have a product which could be adapted for special interest holidays, these magazines are very useful.

The tourist boards publish a plethora of publications. Advertising in these is usually reasonably priced but the angle of many of them is to offer information rather than persuasion. This is not necessarily bad – many holiday makers consult guides as a cross reference before deciding where to book.

When you have obtained media packs and information about relevant publications, use the following criteria to draw up a short list:

Profile of readership

Do the readers correspond to your target markets? The readership profile should detail readers in terms of age and socio-economic profile, as well as giving further details about hobbies and interests, and any research about holiday-taking habits. Tourism products are a major source of revenue for many publications so they will usually have more detailed information available if you ask for it.

Readership

Most publications will give their circulation and readership figures. The readership figures are more interesting because these show the actual number of people who will see and read the publication, not just buy it. For some publications there will be a big difference between the circulation and readership figures. Some of the more upmarket monthly magazines have relatively low circulation figures but a long shelf life and high readership figures – particularly when they are the types of publication you see in doctors' and dentists' surgeries!

When considering readership figures, look also at the distribution method for the publication. Is it one which people really demand, by buying it at a newsagents or requesting it from a tourist information centre? Or one which arrives unrequested through the letterbox?

Publication date

You will need to plan ahead and choose publications whose copy dates you can meet. Even more important are publication dates. If most people plan and book their holiday with you in November, there is little point advertising in a publication which appears in May, unless it is tactical advertising and you are looking for top-up business.

The media pack will probably include details of forthcoming features which might be relevant to you. Sometimes it is a good idea to advertise within a relevant feature but remember that competitors will probably be doing the same. It can be useful to stand alone and make a bigger impact at another time, if the timing is right for you.

Advertising rates

The deciding factor will inevitably be whether or not you can afford to advertise in your chosen publications and if it is cost-effective. Set your budget in advance and stick to it. You might decide to place your advertising through an agency which should not actually cost you anything because they will take a commission from the publications, and may already have special rates.

Whether you book through an agency or place advertisements direct, always try to negotiate a discount. This may be a first-timer's discount, series discount or just because your advertising budget is too small. Regard advertising rate cards as guidelines only. You can negotiate discounts of as much as 50 per cent. When placing advertisements always ask if there is any chance of editorial coverage and the name of the person you should contact.

Benefits and relative merits of different advertising media

Television

▨ Excels in reaching the mass consumer market.

▨ Allows companies to keep product and brand presence in front of customers.

▨ Influences the mass consumer market to long-term conversion to a particular product.

▨ Enables the promotion of corporate image nationwide.

▨ Is made more powerful by the combination of sound, colour and movement.

Press

▨ Allows specific socio-economic groups to be reached.

▨ Allows specific geographical regions to be reached.

▨ Allows more complicated messages to be conveyed.

▦ Is less expensive than television.

Radio

▦ Good for geographical targeting.

▦ Can reach identifiable market segments (youth, those at home during the day).

▦ Costs of radio advertising are relatively low so repetition is easier.

Cinema

▦ Good for reaching the youth market.

▦ Good for consumer segment targeting.

▦ Good scope to use the impact of movement and sound.

▦ Geographically separate markets can also be catered for.

Posters

▦ Good for specific targets (shoppers, etc).

▦ Low cost.

National daily

▦ Expensive.

▦ Only suitable for large multiple chains with nationwide customers.

Provincial daily

▦ Good for local markets.

Evening locals

▦ Good 'opportunity to see' (OTS) figures.

▦ High local coverage.

▦ High readership.

Weekly locals

▦ High local coverage.

▦ Good readership over a period of seven days.

▦ Many OTS.

▦ Good for those at home during the day, senior citizens and long-term residents.

Trade magazines

▦ Good for specific market segments.

Country magazines

▦ Up market.

▦ Good for high socio-economic groups.

▦ High number of readers per copy (ie in doctors' waiting rooms).

▦ Retained over a period of time.

Monthly/weekly magazines

▦ Good for specific target segments.

▦ Tend to be looked at more than once, by various members of the household.

Evaluating advertising campaigns

You will never find out which half of your advertising budget was a good investment unless you monitor it. Keep a record of the media in which you advertised, when and the cost. Make sure that all staff are aware of the need to monitor advertising expenditure and ask them to make a point of asking people who book with you where they heard about you, and to make a note of this.

You can also monitor which publications work for you by using different types of advertisement, such as specific packages or codes when people are asked to complete tear-off vouchers for further information.

Monitoring advertising campaigns is more difficult for destinations and attractions where people simply turn up. Whenever possible you should conduct brief visitor surveys (using students on work placements is an easy way of doing this) questioning representative groups or people at different times of the year.

You will be able to increase the effectiveness of any advertising if it is carefully thought through and planned in advance. Advertising should also be integrated into the marketing plan so activities can be dovetailed. You will raise more awareness of your product if advertising coincides with a PR and direct mail campaign.

Advertising terms

The advertising world uses quite a lot of jargon which it is useful to understand. The majority of publications and programmes will provide a rate card so you can gauge the value for money which they offer. These are some of the terms you are likely to come across:

- *Audited circulation*: The number of copies of a newspaper or magazine sold for an average issue over a stated period.

- *Readership*: The number of people who claim to have read or looked at an average issue of a newspaper or magazine.

- *Readers per copy*: The average number of people who read an issue of a newspaper or magazine.

- *OTS: The Opportunity to See* is the frequency of people's reading or looking at an average issue of a newspaper or magazine, ie if you read three out of six issues of a daily paper and there is an advertisement on six consecutive issues, then you have had three OTS.

Radio and television companies also provide information about their viewers and listeners, using different terms:

▓ *Audience*: The number of people who had an OTS of watching a programme or advertisement.

▓ *Ratings*: The percentage of homes switched to a commercial TV station at a particular time. These ratings are measured in Television Rating Points (TVRs) and it is possible to state how many TVRs any advert gets.

▓ *Coverage*: The proportion of the target population having the OTS at least one advertisement.

▓ *Frequency*: The frequency of the OTS for any campaign.

USING THE INTERNET

As a promotional tool, the Internet is a new and highly powerful medium which cannot be ignored. It should not be seen as a replacement for other promotional activities, but as an expansion of existing ones, which gives consumers greater choice and booking options.

For a relatively low investment of resources, a worldwide audience of intelligent and affluent people can be reached. It is also a very fast-growing and changing medium. Rather than give detailed descriptions and recommendations, this chapter aims to give an overview of the Internet's main features as they are at present.

There are almost daily developments, with which you will need to keep up to date. To find out about the latest developments read some of the expanding range of Internet magazines (many of which are designed for beginners) now appearing in newsagents. Most tourist boards also have staff with a growing knowledge of the Internet so you could turn to them for initial advice.

Needless to say, the Internet has also given rise to a vast army of technology consultants who can offer you advice. Most of them are still learning about the industry too. If you use a consultant, it is probably best to rely on personal recommendations in order to choose someone who can help you.

The Internet is currently growing at around 120 per cent and this figure is growing exponentially. It has been estimated that by the year 2001 over 400 million people will have access to the

Internet. By the year 2005 almost every person in the developed world is likely to have access in some way. This will probably not be in quite the same way as at present, but using far higher speed mass-market methods.

What is the Internet?

It is a complex international network of computers. Data information is held in digital form in vast databases and is accessible by users anywhere in the world. Part of the Internet's power is the software which allows users to download, upload, send and receive information in a minimum time.

There are presently two methods of information exchange which businesses and individuals can use. *E-mail* or electronic mail is developing rapidly and will probably continue to do so in the same way as fax machines did in the mid-1980s, until almost every business has one. The second method is the *World Wide Web* (WWW or the Web), which is a collection of easy to use, graphical pages. This is the fastest growing part of the Internet.

The WWW began at CERN in France, the high energy physics laboratories, in 1989. The Web was created to allow scientists around the world to communicate their ideas more easily. The process of embedding information behind a highlighted word or graphic is called hypertext. This then makes it possible to point and click a computer mouse on that word to uncover the information, making it as easy to use as the average word processor. Before that users needed to use long lines of computer code to transfer information.

An application called a *browser* is used to access the WWW and find relevant sites.

How is the Internet being used?

At present Internet users are primarily aged between 17 and 45, and in higher income brackets. The majority of users are male but the profile of users is broadening and is likely to become more balanced between the sexes very soon.

All that is needed to use the Internet is a computer, modem, telephone line and a subscription to an access provider. The main barriers to use are the cost of equipment and the time it can take to 'go on-line'. However, the costs of both equipment and telephone charges are falling and new technology is making access faster and faster.

Using the Internet as a promotional tool

Organisations who simply replicate their standard print material are unlikely to be as successful as those who develop information with the express purpose of using Web pages. Unlike traditional print media, the Internet does not access information sequentially. Users do not have pages presented automatically to them. They have to search for they want so use is more proactive and users can browse through different sites and pages, switching from one to another. The Internet also makes use of animated graphics and sound to bring Web pages alive.

Addresses of Web sites are known as *URLs* or universal resource locators. For example, an address could be 'http://www.disney.com'. *http* tells the computer that the page is written in *hyper text transfer protocol* format. www stands for World Wide Web. The following part is the company name, followed by an abbreviation which indicates the type of organisation. *com or co.uk* indicates that it is a company, *org* is a non-profit making organisation and *edu* is an educational establishment.

Users obviously need to find Web addresses in order to use the Web site. Web site developers can publicise their addresses by printing them on letterheads and brochures, and by registering them with *search engines*. These are services such as Yahoo, which is effectively a contents page for the Internet, and works by searching their databases for key words which the user has input.

Promotional opportunities on the Internet

Using the Internet as a promotional tool has several advantages:

▓ It can reach a mass audience right in their place of work or home.

▓ You can use animated graphics, pictures, short films, text and sound to deliver your message – in this way the Internet is more similar to television than print material.

▓ You can monitor usage of Web sites, and even obtain quite detailed data about users.

▓ It can offer a channel of distribution as well as a channel of communication, with the chance to book on-line.

However the Internet is likely to lead to increased competition between some products. This is more likely to affect retailers offering homogeneous products than the tourism industry, but will have some effect. Automatic search programmes can search sites for specific products and then report back where the cheapest can be found – worldwide. They will convert prices into local currencies, and even add on import duties and delivery costs.

Price is not always a determining factor for the choice of destination but it is for some tourism services such as car hire. Using the Internet it is now possible to book car hire through offices in the USA where prices are more competitive, and to pick up the car from a local base.

Hotels, tour operators and destinations will benefit from more imaginative and practical presentation of their products. Users will be able to download video images of facilities and destinations so they can see before they buy.

The Internet is particularly useful for last minute bookings because it is possible to buy products on-line and directly, when booking agents and receptions are closed.

Advertising on the Internet is becoming increasingly sophisticated. Vast amounts of information can be gathered about Internet users, based on the types of sites which they access most frequently, such as their interests and usage patterns. For the first time advertisements will be created immediately for a very specific audience.

For example, the search engines load an advertisement to match the search required by the user. If you were looking for holidays in Cornwall, the search engine can generate an advertisement for accommodation there. The advertisement could be even more specific depending on the information requested.

Another promotional opportunity is that of developing a Web site so that users can access information about your product directly.

Creating Web sites

Setting up a new Web site is relatively inexpensive and quick to do. All you need to do is:

▓ Register your site, so that host computers know where to find it.

▓ Buy web space (many Internet providers offer a certain amount free of charge) in the same way as you book advertising space.

▓ Develop the actual site and make sure it is kept up to date.

The format and design of the web site will be crucial to its success, as well as ensuring the search engines can find it. Web sites should be designed independently of traditional print media, although the same logos and branding can be used. The Internet offers the opportunity to bring the experience of your product alive, with sound and pictures. You should use this, as well as making sure that your Web site links with other relevant ones.

The approach which is to be avoided at all costs, is that of developing sites which resemble the classified lists of some directories. Users access the Internet in a different way to traditional brochures and if your home page does not catch their attention and hold their interest they will browse others instead. Travel excites the senses. Bland text does not give the same opportunity to sample travel experiences as sound-bites and moving images.

Once a user has looked at your Web site, they may be ready to make a booking. Simply giving addresses and telephone numbers for them to use is not enough. You should take advantage of the opportunities offered by the Internet and make it easy for people to request further information or book. This means offering on-line request and booking facilities which make it both easy and immediate.

Experience in France with the Minitel system (which is a similar service to the Internet but was set up several years ago) has shown that there is huge potential to sell products directly to travellers in their own homes. The Minitel network already accounts for a substantial number of travel reservations in France.

The Internet will be particularly useful for accessing markets with a high propensity towards independent travel. Independent travel is growing rapidly. As they become more experienced travellers, visitors to tourism destinations increasingly want to customise their holiday to suit themselves. The Internet offers them this opportunity. Sites which link related products and offer loose packages (ie the opportunity to mix and match individual components) will be successful.

If you want to develop more information about users of your Web site, you will need to make them offers or give incentives which are only available there, to encourage them to register their details with you.

You can also use the Internet to save resources. Tourism organisations are increasingly using touch tone voice mail systems to deal with standard enquiries and bookings. These can be accessed day and night and allow the public to obtain information relatively quickly and easily.

You can use the Internet in the same way, cutting down on staff time to answer standard enquiries and on the need for some brochures. For example, if you receive the same routine requests and questions about things such as opening times, prices, how to reach you, etc, you can develop part of your site to provide that information.

Key points to build Web sites that generate new and additional business

▓ The Internet needs different forms of information to standard print. Simply adapting plain text for the Internet is not effective

– information needs to be developed specifically for the Internet.

▓ The Internet makes good use of sound and animation. However you should not rely on these gimmicks alone. You will need to present information which is persuasive and relevant. Make the information enjoyable and entertaining to access so users become involved in your site and do not drift off to others.

▓ It is important to use imaginative and persuasive packaging, perhaps linking accommodation and attractions. You can increase the level and value of bookings if you anticipate users' needs.

▓ For example, if users consistently request information about major attractions and you have other equally good attractions with low visitor numbers, you can present the two together, using the larger to sell the smaller.

▓ You could take this a step further. If a visitor goes to two attractions on one day, they will probably also want refreshments. You could develop a third-party promotion and increase visitor numbers at both attractions, by offering a combined package of entrance to both attractions and refreshment vouchers.

▓ It is essential to provide booking links – people will only buy if it is easy for them to do so.

▓ There is a further opportunity to increase the value of tourism to your area. You can offer links to other sites which promote and sell high-quality merchandise, and which reinforces the identity of your destination.

DIRECT MAIL

In some circles, direct mail or 'junk mail' has developed a negative reputation. This is mainly due to the vast number of badly written, untargeted letters which are churned out. When it is done well, direct mail is a successful and cost-effective promotional tool. Good direct mail is about sending precise sales messages directly to potential or existing customers in their home or office. Similar results can be achieved using e-mail and faxes as by letters.

Direct mail has many advantages. It addresses individuals by name so it can be highly targeted. You can buy or develop mailing lists and select targets by their job, postcode, income level or interests.

Direct mail is extremely flexible. It is often assumed that mail-shots have to be to huge numbers of people, but they could equally be to just a dozen. You can also experiment, by sending out different types of letters to different targets, to see which is most productive.

Monitoring direct mail is also easier than most promotional methods. You will know exactly to whom you have written so you can assess responses very accurately.

Response rates of around 1 per cent for mailing lists which you have hired and rates of up to 7 per cent for previous customers may sound very low. However, the actual cost of reaching those people is also low compared to other promotional activities. Response rates can be increased using a carefully researched list, good letter and offer and mechanisms such as response paid reply cards which make responding easier.

Direct mail can be very creative. You could just send a letter or you could send cards or other items. For example, several resorts have sent small packets of sand with their letters to potential visitors, reminding them of the feel of the beach. Holiday destinations can use picture postcards with messages which look like they have been hand-written, to great effect.

Humour is also useful. A leading incentive agency was asked to develop a campaign which would increase sales at a national chain of car dealerships. An incentive trip 'of a lifetime' was to be the prize for the top ten salespeople in the chain. The incentive agency needed to tell all the salespeople about the competition, and use that communication as an opportunity to motivate them.

They sent humorous letters out to all the salespeople at their home addresses, telling them the incentive agency had been retained to find ways of motivating the sales force. The letter attracted the salespeople's attention because of its quirky, tongue-in-cheek style which intimated that the agency had been told that this motivation campaign might be a real challenge. At the end of the letter the agency said they were still working on some ideas and would be in touch very shortly.

Two days later each salesperson received a box carrot, with a short message. It said the agency were working on a really 'big idea' which they were sure would be very exciting to all the sales-force. They could not reveal details yet, but suggested that the salespeople should start to work really hard to achieve their targets, and hoped that they preferred a carrot to a stick. More details would be revealed in a few days.

A few days later each of the salespeople received a hand-written postcard posted from the incentive destination, which acted as an invitation to join the competition. This was followed by details of the incentive competition. All the salespeople were talking about the campaign, morale was high and sales soared.

You will not necessarily need to use such a protracted or expensive campaign to get results. Thinking laterally and using humour are good approaches to use.

Developing mailing lists

Good lists give good results. You will need to either buy a mailing list or develop one yourself. Whichever you choose, ensure it is an absolute maximum of two years old. Lists which have been cleaned more recently to reduce duplications, errors and people who have moved will be more effective and reduce your postage costs.

Lists of your previous visitors or guests are very useful. Not only can you perhaps persuade some of them to come back to you, you can use the list as a basis for developing new ones. You can have your list analysed by direct mail specialists to find out the profile of your existing customers, based on their post codes. Using computer systems the post codes are matched to data about consumer lifestyles. Once you know what kind of people already enjoy your product it is a relatively easy process to obtain lists of new people with a similar profile who might be interested.

You should think just as carefully about target markets and

segments for direct mail as for any other form of promotion. Direct mail is not particularly good for general awareness raising. It works best in markets which are already quite well-informed about your product or similar ones.

Lists can be borrowed or developed from business directories and trade bodies. The BTA has lists available for hire which give names and contact details for different segments of the travel trade overseas. Your regional tourist board will probably also have some lists which they may make available to you.

If you are trying to attract group business you could develop your own list of local groups and organisations based on area directories and information from your local library and local authorities.

There are numerous list brokers who sell lists which can be divided by geographic region, profession, interest, age and so on. They usually have a minimum order of about 1000 names, which generally cost around £75–£100 per 1000. These types of lists may be particularly good if you wish to promote special interest holidays or have identified a particular profession as having strong potential for your product.

The Royal Mail is a useful source of information and free advice about direct mail and will often recommend good mailing houses and brokers.

If you keep your mailing list on computer, bear in mind that under the Data Protection Act you must register your lists and adhere to the conditions of the Act. You can obtain further information by telephoning the Data Protection Registrar on 01625 545745.

Before you conduct a massive mailing, it is worth testing your mailing list and letter by sending it to only a limited number of addresses. If you do not get a response you will need to improve either the list or the letter.

Developing a sales proposition or offer

Direct mail letters are effectively sales presentations on paper. To grab attention and elicit a positive response you will need to make a strong offer.

Offers which work are not necessarily discounts. During the recession discounts were widely used. As a result we have become immune to many of them – price cuts are no longer news. Added value offers convey a more positive message and will probably cost you less.

You could decide to offer something which is indirectly related to your product or service. For example, if you are promoting winter short breaks for walkers, you could include a free flask which will be filled with a hot drink each morning before they go on their way, or perhaps a free guide to local walks.

You might also use a third-party offer which gives a discount or voucher for another organisation or activity. An attraction could offer groups vouchers giving a £1 discount on all purchases over £5 in the gift shop, or arrange a special package which combines the entrance fee with afternoon tea.

Direct mail is a good medium for sales promotions. These are usually promotions with a specific timescale and clear, short-term objectives. Sales promotions include:

▨ added-value offers;

▨ special discounts;

▨ friend-get-friend offers;

▨ special schemes such as incentives or commission payments for a specific booking period.

Sales promotions are very useful for generating sales in quiet periods, attracting new customers for the first time, and introducing new products. To be successful they must be carefully targeted with a limited time span and genuine offer. It is essential that it is easy to respond and take advantage of the offer.

The offer which you include in your direct mail letter might not be an offer in the sense of a sales promotion. Solutions to problems or promises work equally well. People may not be buying for obvious reasons. Consider someone looking for a hotel room. They do not just book hotel rooms because they are looking for somewhere to sleep. They book because they are looking for a break with routine, romance or to be near a famous sight or place.

A good way of looking at your product or service from a customer point of view is to speak to existing guests or visitors. Ask them:

▓ What is it about place/product/package you like?

▓ Why did you buy it in the first place?

▓ What attracted your attention to it?

▓ What was/is most appealing to you?

▓ What are the biggest benefits it has given you?

Try to see your product from your customer's perspective and show them a solution to their problems or promise something you know they want, and you can deliver.

Writing successful direct mail letters

Before you write your communication you should give some thought to whether a letter, fax, postcard or e-mail will be the most effective medium. It is useful to have a choice but for many purposes letters offer the most flexibility, although faxes are useful if you want to communicate with businesses. In some countries where the postal system is not particularly reliable, faxes are also useful for communicating with consumers. This is especially the case in Japan and the BTA office there offers various fax-based promotional opportunities.

You will find writing direct mail letters easier and more effective if you follow these key steps:

1. Use a hook to grab attention. This could be an intriguing headline or a question to which the answer is almost certainly yes. For example, if you are a hotel offering short breaks for couples you might start with, 'Would you like to put an extra touch of romance in your life?'

2. The second part of your letter should give some further information which reinforces your earlier question or headline, and gives the details of your 'offer'. The second para-

graph or sentence should follow on naturally from the first so the reader is encouraged to continue reading.

3. At this point many readers will have become cynical and either started to think the offer is too good to be true or there is some catch. You will need to offer reassurance or a further explanation, followed with more information about the offer.

4. The final section should push the reader to take action. This could be by using a response-paid coupon, tear-off slip, voucher or simply stating a telephone number for bookings. Giving a deadline for action is also effective.

The first impression created by the envelope in which you send your letter is important. Brown paper envelopes are marginally cheaper than white or coloured ones but they look cheap. Window envelopes remind people of bills so although they are practical, they can be off-putting. It is a good idea to check what is printed on your franking machine if you have one and investigate the possibility of changing its message to something which relates to the mail shot.

Intrigue works well. If you can use intrigue on your envelope or in the first sentence of your letter you will have already involved your reader. This does not mean overprinting your envelope with 'Open Now!!! Special Offer Inside!!!' That approach has been over-used. In these days of franking machines and word processors, hand-written envelopes and proper stamps are most likely to attract attention but they are time-consuming to produce.

General copy-writing tips for direct mail letters

Using these tips will help you to write better direct mail letters:

▓ Make sure you start with the target's name. If you do not have one use another relevant name such as 'Dear walker' or 'Dear worn-out city dweller' instead of Dear Sir or Madam.

▓ Use a warm, friendly style. Remember to keep a picture of a typical reader in your mind so you write a personalised letter rather than one which is aimed at 2000 people.

▨ Read your letter aloud to make sure it does not sound stilted.

▨ Try to keep your letter to one side of A4 – if it looks longer recipients may be put off reading it.

▨ A PS at the end of the letter will usually attract attention, particularly if it reinforces the sales message.

▨ Use techniques such as underlining or emboldening to stress important elements of the letter. CAPITAL LETTERS ARE MORE DIFFICULT TO READ.

▨ Make sure you include a deadline for response. If you give an incentive such as '10 per cent discount if you book before December', you will also increase response rates.

▨ Remember to make your sales letter customer-oriented. Use 'you' rather than 'I' or 'we'.

You can test out response rates by changing different elements of the letter. For example, in one batch of letters you could change your headline or opening sentence. In another you could change the offer you make to see if this makes a difference to response levels. Before you send out your letter test it on colleagues or even existing customers and ask them what their response would be or how it could be improved.

Budgeting for direct mail

Do not fall into the trap of only working out how much postage will cost for your direct mail campaign. You will need to take into consideration:

▨ list purchase or time taken to clean or develop existing lists;

▨ stationery (which may need to be specially printed);

▨ envelopes;

▨ labels or time to write addresses;

▨ postage;

▒ time for stuffing envelopes;

▒ any reply mechanism;

▒ cost of any offer you make as part of the direct mail campaign.

The Royal Mail will provide discounted postage rates on large-scale mailings if your mail shot is pre-sorted by postcode. For further details speak to the manager of your local Royal Mail office.

Monitoring your direct mail campaign

You will already know how much your campaign has cost and how many people you wrote to. You will need to make a daily note of responses, and whether they were converted from enquiries into bookings. If you work out the total value of the business generated you will be able to calculate the financial return on your direct mail campaign.

Alternatively you may decide that the rewards are greater than just direct financial ones, having introduced new customers to your organisation who may return more than once and pass on positive word of mouth recommendations to other people.

If you are disappointed by the results of your direct mail campaign, do not give up. Direct mail is a useful medium and it works well for many businesses. You probably need to take another look at your mailing lists, letters or the offer you make.

Finally, do not just look at your own organisation for inspiration. Start to collect examples of direct mail which you receive and analyse which parts of it you think are successful and why so you can copy some of the better ideas.

SALES ACTIVITIES

Face-to-face selling is one of the best ways of promoting any product. Because it is so personalised, the sales presentation can be adapted to suit the audience and people are far more persuasive than paper promotions. Selling means actually taking an order or booking so sales activities are relatively easy to monitor.

In the past only businesses like attractions and hotels under-took sales activities. Destinations restricted their direct sales efforts to exhibitions. Now some destinations are beginning to find that by actually visiting tour and coach operators and making a sales presentation they can directly influence operators to feature their destination. They can then go back to hoteliers and attractions in their area with details of prime contacts who are ready to make bookings.

Personal sales are very effective, but they must be planned and targeted like any other promotion. The good news is that almost anyone can develop sales skills.

Developing sales skills

A good salesperson is not just good at selling. They need to have a sound understanding of the tourism industry and excellent product knowledge. If you are going to undertake sales calls you will need to develop a detailed understanding of not just your own product but also that of your competitors. It is important to know the relative strengths and weaknesses of competitor's products and services.

You can find sales leads and ideas for new product develop-ment by visiting exhibitions, reading the trade press and being aware of other aspects of the tourism industry outside your own area. A friendly, enthusiastic personality will help you sell, but there is no substitute for carefully researched information and a structured approach to sales activities.

Sources of business

The main target for your sales activities will probably be members of the travel trade. You will need to develop a list of potential 'prospects' using whichever sources are most relevant for you.

You should be able to develop a list of people to call on from the following:

- By keeping lists of previous clients. If they have visited once they may come back again or send other visitors to you. Just because someone has enjoyed your product once do not rely on them to come back – they will need to be reminded. Existing clients could also refer other business to you.

- Trade associations such as the British Incoming Tour Operators' Association.

- The trade press, especially using information about new companies and staff moves.

- Exhibitions.

- Mailing lists, particularly those supplied by your regional tourist board or the British Tourist Authority.

When you develop your list of sales prospects make sure they fit in with your target markets. Prioritise markets and contacts and set targets for when you will visit them. Decide in advance which products or packages you will promote to them. This will help you to integrate sales activities into your promotional programme.

Making appointments

The first time you telephone someone and try to make an appointment with them can be daunting. You will feel more confident if you have jotted down what you plan to say to them and thought about the benefits you want to present. Do not launch into a full sales spiel when you telephone someone. Your aim should be to get them to spare a few minutes for you to see them, when you will be able to present your product much more effectively than on the telephone.

You will need to make sure that you see someone who has responsibility for booking or selecting new products. Within tour operators this is usually the role of the contracts manager but in smaller companies people are less likely to have titles. If you are trying to get a tour operator to feature your destination or product for the first time you might also find it helpful to speak to people involved in marketing because they will have a better idea of what their clients are looking for and what sells.

Find out relevant contact names in advance. If you do not have them, telephone and ask who is responsible for contracting or marketing, then try to make an appointment with them.

If you feel that a secretary is blocking your call do not leave your number and ask them to ring back. They probably will not. Ask the secretary when is the best time to call and call back then.

You will find it easier to make appointments if you have a concrete reason for the sales meeting. For example, if you have launched a new service or package or perhaps got some special rates for tour operators.

Be proactive and suggest a time to meet. By suggesting a time like quarter to three you will sound like you are organised and busy and you only have a limited amount of time which will reassure the person you are trying to meet. It is useful to say that you think the meeting will only take about half an hour so it does not sound like you will waste their time. If you have given a time limit for the sales meeting make sure you stick to it.

Some people will ask you to send them information rather than going to see them. If all else fails and you really do not think they are very interested, then do this. But it is much better to tell them you need to find out more information about their business so you can give them relevant information and rates.

Planning the sales meeting

Do not just take along a handful of brochures and photographs and turn up at the sales meeting. Plan it so you can really get something out of it, even if it is information instead of a sale.

Before you go to the meeting:

⬚ Think what you already know about the potential client. What can you find out about them? Consider what they need and how you can satisfy that need. You will have to tailor your sales presentation to suit different types of client. For example, a mainstream tour operator may wish to know that you can handle large groups efficiently whereas someone booking educational travel may be more concerned about safety and educational value.

▓ Make sure you have defined your Unique Selling Point and developed a list of real benefits for that client. Consider what those benefits will mean to your potential client and the best way of presenting them.

▓ Think about the possible objections which the client might raise, and consider how you can overcome them.

Overcoming objections

You will not be able to foresee or overcome all objections. However, you can think about some of them in advance and decide how you will handle them. This way you will be more confident and ready to deal with any objections.

Here are some common objections or delaying tactics and how to deal with them.

'I need to speak to Mr X before I can make a decision'

Ask when they will be speaking to Mr X and say you will call them shortly after. Or ask if you can speak to Mr X directly.

'I'm not sure' or 'I do not know'

The client is not raising a tangible objection. They are just not sure and need convincing – continue to sell to them.

'The price is too high'

Do not start to negotiate a lower price straightaway. Try to explain why the price is as high as it is. Do not apologise because this means you also think the price is expensive. Some of the ways of counteracting objections about high prices can seem flippant but they will help you to establish if the objection is a real one or just part of the usual sales sequence.

Try telling the client that cheaper products are not as good. Or that your product really does offer good value for money. Another way is to offer to let the client try your product for themselves because you are sure they will then appreciate that it is really good value for money.

If the client raises several objections during the course of your meeting it could be that they are really not interested in what you are selling. It could also mean that this is just part of their usual technique. You will probably find that some of the objections are gestures rather than real objections.

Try to analyse and prioritise the objections, rather than locking yourself into a discussion of all of them. Make sure you put any problems into perspective. You can even turn the objection round by asking how you could help the client to solve the problem or overcome the objection.

Make sure you stress the advantages and benefits once again so the disadvantages are minimised.

Reasons why people buy

It is worth considering some of the reasons people buy products. If you are aware of these and can identify which are important to your client, you will be able to give appropriate sales messages.

As many as 85 per cent of all decisions are said to be based on emotion, not logic. We do not always buy products for obvious reasons. We buy products for/out of:

▨ prestige;
▨ greed;
▨ pride;
▨ ego;
▨ ambition;
▨ status;
▨ fun;
▨ security;
▨ fear.

Take a look at some of the advertisements in glossy magazines and on television. Consider the products which are being promoted and the messages they use. Few of them even mention the advantages of the product. They focus on benefits and other reasons for buying, implying for example that if we buy that lipstick we will look as good as the model wearing it, and our life will be so much better.

Structure for the sales meeting

Do not go into the sales meeting and give a quick run through the wonders of your product. Plan and structure the meeting so you are in control.

Initial greeting

It is easy to start a sales meeting with a grumble about the weather or traffic. This is supposed to break the ice, but presents a negative message right from the start. Another bad opening line is 'I was just passing so I thought I'd come to see you'. This conveys the impression that you do not attribute much importance or priority to the client.

Start with a simple friendly greeting and thank the client for sparing their time to see you. Reassure them that you will not take up more than x minutes of their time. They will think you are business-like and they can relax and focus on what you have to say.

Initial sales statement

You need to have their full attention. Make an initial sales statement so they will want to listen to you, before you go on to ask questions about their business. For example, 'I think you will be interested in our new package for tour operators like yourself – but first I just need to ask a few questions to make sure I'm selling you the right product'.

Bear in mind that most potential buyers will be thinking 'What's in it for me?' You will have their attention if you imply you can offer them something of direct benefit. They do not like time-wasters so make sure the sales meeting is structured and directed.

Questions

This is your opportunity to find out more about the client's business and their needs so you can angle your sales presentation appropriately.

Sales presentation

You should have prepared your sales presentation earlier but do not let it sound like a scripted presentation which you have delivered ten times already that week. Make sure that you vary your voice and tone and ensure you focus on the benefits your product can offer. People buy people so try to be human and maintain eye contact.

Visual aids such as photographs will help the client to focus on what you are saying and to imagine your product if they are not already familiar with it.

If you use the sort of flip-over table-top presenter which has photographs or sales points for the client to see, you might find it helpful to include identical pages facing you so you can read them or comment on them without turning the presenter away from the client and losing eye contact with them.

Ask questions as you deliver your presentation and respond to any perceived reservations which the client may have.

Watch out for buying signals and make sure you recognise them. Some people find it difficult to stop talking and are so intent on delivering their prepared presentation they do not notice that the client is trying to book!

Recognising buying signals

The client's body language is one way of judging how interested they are. If they cross their arms and leave them that way, you can be fairly certain you are not getting through to them. More open, positive body language such as nods of understanding and approval mean you are saying what they want to hear.

Any enquiries about prices or requests for more details about your product are effectively buying signals. All you need to do is deliver the right answer so they can buy. Even minor worries or reservations are buying signals because they indicate that if you remove those, the way will be clear for you to do business together.

Towards the end of your presentation or when you have recognised good buying signals you should start to make some minor assumptions. These might include asking if the client would like you to arrange credit facilities for them, or asking which of their clients would most enjoy your product.

At this stage you may find that they once again raise some small objections. Stress the benefits and be open with the client. Ask them if they would be ready to book with you if you can sort out those minor problems.

Once you have finished your presentation do not be afraid of asking for bookings, or asking whether they are likely to be working with you in the near future. Do not chatter to break a silence. When faced with a short pause or silence, many people will use the occasion to buy!

Experiencing your product at first-hand will help to convince the client and seal a future bond between you. Offer to arrange for them to sample it, either alone or with their family. You should either set a date there and then, or send complimentary tickets or vouchers to them as soon as possible.

Before you leave make sure you have agreed what the follow up to the meeting will be. Do not just leave with a vague, 'I'll look forward to hearing from you'. This puts the ball in the client's court and is not very positive. If you can agree that you will take specific action by a certain date you will have another chance to impress with your efficiency and the sale will once again be in your hands.

EXHIBITIONS

Exhibitions are useful, not just as an exhibitor. They are worth going to, to gather information about competitors and to find out more about general market trends. If you are considering going to an exhibition as an exhibitor, try to go before as a non-exhibitor to learn out more about its format, or at least speak to people who have exhibited there before.

The exhibition industry is developing. In some countries the exhibition culture is already very well established. Go to one of the public exhibitions in Germany where people gather as much information as possible before booking a holiday, and you will find people actually queuing at the door before the exhibition opens.

Choosing exhibitions to attend

There are of course differences between public and trade exhibitions, and indeed between exhibitions in different countries. Exhibitions offer an excellent opportunity to make new contacts and promote your product to a wider public.

Your regional tourist board and the BTA will be able to tell you more about the range of exhibitions available. Some of the most prominent ones are:

October	MITCAR, Paris	trade
November	World Travel Market, London	trade
January	Fitur, Madrid	trade, some public
January	CMT, Stuttgart	public
January	Holiday World, Dublin	public, some trade
February	OP PAD, Netherlands	public
February	BIT, Milan	trade
February	Reisen, Hamburg	public
February	CBR Munich	public
March	ITB, Berlin	trade
March	TUR, Gothenburg	trade, some public
March	British Travel Trade Fair	trade

The dates given are approximate as some of them vary slightly from year to year. There are also many smaller regional exhibitions such as the 'day out fairs' like 'Excursions' in South East England organised by some of the regional tourist boards, which are particularly suitable for attractions and destinations.

If you do decide to take a stand at an exhibition, do your homework. Is it in the right area or country to attract your target market? Will it attract consumers or the travel trade? What format is it? Some exhibitions such as TUR in Gothenburg are a combination of public and trade days. Others, like the massive trade show, ITB in Berlin work on a completely different basis, and if you do not already have established contacts with whom you can make appointments in advance, it is not worth attending.

Consider the level of awareness of your product in your chosen markets. If it is not high you will probably find exhibition attendance is more productive if you join together with other

British products to make a stronger impact. Exhibiting under the BTA umbrella can be useful in these circumstances.

Exhibiting is expensive and there are a lot of additional expenses which you will need to take into consideration. In addition to the exhibition space you will need to budget for the stand itself, display material, possible additional costs for carpets, chairs, tables and lighting, travel to and from the exhibition as well as subsistence.

Sharing a stand will obviously be cheaper but it might also make your stand more attractive to potential visitors. In less well-established markets you will benefit from combining with other suppliers. For example, a stand on which a hotel, attraction and destination are represented will be more useful to visitors, because they can offer a readily packaged product, making it easier to buy.

Always ask exhibition organisers what promotional opportunities and facilities are included in the price. Many offer good PR opportunities through their own press office, and organise affiliated conferences in which you might be able to take part.

Setting objectives

Why do you want to exhibit? To raise awareness of your destination or product? To make new trade contacts or refresh existing ones? To actually sign contracts and take bookings? Whatever your reason, do not just content yourself with considering exhibition attendance as a 'useful PR exercise'. If all exhibitions do is offer an opportunity to network and swop stories with colleagues and visitors, you can surely find cheaper ways of doing so.

Like many other promotional activities, it can be difficult to evaluate the effectiveness of exhibition attendance. It will be easier to monitor particular exhibitions, and you will generate more visitors if you can identify a real purpose for your attendance.

This should not just be the basic objective of raising awareness or making new contacts, but one with identifiable results. You could launch a new product, 'unveil' a new brochure, or promote a special package. For example, a hotel may join forces with a local attraction and offer an all-in price.

Whatever you decide, do make sure that it is different in some way. If you look through the articles in the trade press shortly before world travel market, you will see how many new brochures are launched. Most of these will simply be updates on the previous year's brochure with a few new photographs and price increases. Try to think of a new angle, service or something which really gives added value – and promote it.

Another idea for attractions or destinations is to offer a free guide book or piece of information which is costly to mail and for which you would normally make a charge, but which nonetheless promotes your product. You can usually think of something which you could give away free at exhibitions. Many exhibitors give sweets or free pencils but it is far more beneficial to give something with real value, which you promote in advance of the exhibition. This will detract some of the free-loaders but still attract more visitors than if you do not offer anything.

If you have a tangible promotion you will be able to judge how many people requested, or showed interest in it and be able to follow that through and look at increased booking levels.

You will need to make sure that all pre-show publicity mentions your special promotion. This could include advertisements (remember to make sure they are in publications well before the exhibition date) or press releases which state your stand number and the promotion. Direct mail can be effective but bear in mind that operators and members of the travel trade are usually deluged by direct mail letters just before exhibitions. You will need to make yours different to attract attention.

Stand design

Some exhibitors try to convey every possible sales message on their exhibition stand, displaying a variety of images without conveying a strong impression of anything. Two or three high quality good big photographs or straplines are far more effective than a vague fan-like display of different leaflets. Make an impact.

Think in advance what the target market is and what message they are most interested in reading. Make sure your display material conveys that message and try not to crowd it by offering other images as well. Make sure the photographs convey your strong points. Alternatively grab visitors' attention by showing images or shots that they might not expect to see.

Dressing staff in costume is not appropriate for all exhibitions and can look gimmicky but it can still work. Costumes do not have to be extreme – they could be more of a uniform.

One of the most striking (and cost-effective) exhibition stands I have seen was a tour operator who used only black and white posters to decorate their stand. Each of these was a panel describing key benefits of their company and highlights of some of their tours, reversed out so the text was white on black. All the exhibition staff wore black trousers and black and white sweat-shirts bearing the name of the company.

If you have one strong sales message and can attract people to the stand, you will have an opportunity to tell them about other aspects of your product.

Selecting staff for the exhibition

Your choice of exhibition staff will be important. They need to have sufficient stature and experience to negotiate and present information effectively, but they must also be energetic and enthusiastic, and above all, good at dealing with people, particularly if you are going to a public exhibition. Your managing director may be important but does he or she have a ready smile and endless patience in dealing with the public? At the other end of the scale, beware choosing pretty faces who draw people to the stand and who then lose sales because their product knowledge is inadequate.

If the exhibition is overseas, it is essential to send people who speak relevant languages. Do not just assume everyone speaks English because it is a world language – you are selling so you must make it easy to buy, which usually means selling in the buyer's language.

Before the exhibition, gather stand staff together and run through your objectives with them. Make sure their product knowledge is good and decide on the key sales messages which you want to convey.

Encourage everyone to make notes about the contacts they make. A handful of business cards is always more useful if there are notes on the reverse about each of the businesses and their needs. Get staff to make notes on appropriate follow-up activity, putting stars against any particularly good contacts. Really good salespeople also make a note of the contact's appearance or a key fact about them such as they have two children, love cream cakes or interest in a particular region. This helps when following up contacts, because you can avoid totally standard letters.

Many exhibitions use colour-coded badges for visitors so you can find out what each colour means and then ask relevant questions, or seek out key buyers more easily. Make sure you know what each colour stands for.

Run through your approach with staff beforehand to make sure they use good selling techniques. They should always try to find out more about the products visitors are looking for and about their business. Staff can then outline the main benefits of your product or service, bearing in mind the visitors' earlier comments. It is also useful to consider possible objections so staff are ready to counteract them.

Visitors to exhibitions are usually looking for information. By coming to the exhibition they are saying that they are willing to buy, either then or later. Exhibitions offer a more relaxed atmosphere than one-to-one sales meetings, and visitors are usually willing to be drawn into conversation. Exhibitions are about striking up contact with total strangers.

You will not get this opportunity very often. Do not ask closed questions like, 'have you been to Never Never Land?' If the answer is yes, you can exchange a few words about the wonderful time they had and if the answer is no, perhaps begin to expound on the virtues of your product. It can be difficult to take this type of conversation further.

You will be more successful if you ask open questions so you can find out information from visitors, and then sell to them. Remember they have come along to gather information and possibly buy so give them the opportunity to do so. Agree what you will do next, such as sending on information or arranging an appointment to see them. Make sure you do it.

Consider also the number of people on the stand. If you have too many, visitors will just feel intimidated and overwhelmed. It is better to have fewer staff on the stand, and let the others take a break so that when they return to the stand, they are fresh and enthusiastic again. Bored and tired exhibitors do not sell anything.

Another important aspect of exhibition attendance is the opportunity for gathering market intelligence. You and your staff can find out what your competitors are doing and obtain copies of their promotional literature. You can also gather information about the general state of the market, and use visitors' comments to improve your service.

At the end of the exhibition swop notes with all the people on your stand, agree who will be responsible for follow-ups and evaluate the exhibition. If you leave this until later, you probably will not do it. I suspect that many exhibitions continue to flourish because they become part of a habit, rather than because they are excellent exhibitions.

If you have any comments about the exhibition organisation, type of visitors or any ideas about how it could be improved, make sure you pass these on to the organisers. They do take notice of these because their success is dependent on attracting good and happy exhibitors.

Sales material

The sales material and information which you take to any exhibition should vary according to the type of exhibition and your objectives. If it is an overseas exhibition you will need to get at least some of the material translated.

If you are going to a trade exhibition, do not expect visitors to take away your thick glossy sales packs with them. They will end up grumpy with tired arms and a tendency to lighten their load by dumping some of the material. There is also no guarantee that once visitors have humped those heavy bags home, all of the material will find its way into their offices. Once in the office carrier bags of exhibition brochures have a habit of staying in a pile on someone's desk and not being used.

It is far better to take just a few comprehensive sales packs with you and to produce a practical fact sheet which outlines all relevant information, and which is tailored to the exhibition. You should then ask for visitor's details and make sure you send the information they actually need, as soon as possible after the exhibition.

This will give you the opportunity to impress potential clients with your efficiency and to build up a database at the same time. Ensure that the information you produce is carefully targeted to the recipient. For example, travel trade visitors will probably want some group rates and details of events up to a year in advance.

Using exhibitions as a PR opportunity

You should make the most of your exhibition attendance by integrating your promotional activities so that the exhibition is part of your PR campaign and vice versa.

Many exhibitions have a publicity questionnaire which is used as the basis for much of the information supplied to the media prior to the show. This results in press coverage and persuades journalists to attend the exhibition. If you receive a publicity questionnaire do not put it in your in-tray – complete it immediately. This is your opportunity for free publicity so use it.

These types of form often ask for a 50 or 100 word description of your activities. When every word counts, these short descriptions can take a long time to draft and get right. It is useful to have a couple you prepared earlier, which you will find you can use for many similar forms.

Draw up your own press list of names of people to contact, and make sure you contact them well in advance of the exhibition. If you are approaching monthly trade magazines, bear in mind that their copy date for the exhibition preview issues may be as much as three or four months in advance. Do not forget to include your local papers in your press list, particularly if you are launching a new product. They like good news stories about local companies and organisations.

Exhibitions seem to give rise to many contrived publicity photographs – but amazingly many get published. Think about a photo opportunity for your organisation.

There will almost certainly be a press office at the exhibition, to which you can deliver your press packs. If you are planning any kind of launch, photo opportunity or special event, make sure you inform the exhibition's publicity officers in advance so they can let other people know about it.

Make sure you deliver supplies of your press pack to the press office just before the beginning of the show. Bear in mind that journalists will not want to pick up every pack. Use a visually attractive folder for your press pack or clear plastic folder and make sure it clearly shows your name and organisation.

Inside the press pack you should include any brief press releases which are geared specifically to the exhibition, any relevant photographs and a brochure if you are launching a new one. Try to keep press pack contents to a minimum so journalists can still manage to carry them!

MARKETING CONSORTIA

Marketing consortia use the synergy of members to raise the profile of the group as a whole. Forming a consortium can help partners to reach their customers more cost-effectively, without losing their independence. By pooling resources, the effect of promotional activities is enhanced and maximised.

Consortia vary in their purpose and types of membership. Some focus on a particular aspect of the tourism industry such as hotels or attractions. Large consortia like Best Western act as a central marketing agency for independent hotels and even offer a central reservations facility. Other consortia are much smaller and perhaps more selective. Treasure Houses of England is a relatively small group of selected historic houses like Beaulieu which produce a joint brochure and take a stand at various exhibitions.

Some consortia serve the interests of members in a specific geographic area, operating in a similar way to tourist boards. They may undertake promotional activities or just act as a trade body to offer each other mutual support. Other consortia are formed with a specific purpose such as trying to develop markets like Japan which are difficult for individual tourism suppliers to access.

Whether they are called partnerships, associations, co-operatives or consortia, these groupings can be powerful if they have clear objectives and adequate resources for their activities.

Benefits and activities of marketing consortia

Consortia develop in different ways to engage in any or all of these activities:

Overseas marketing

Overseas marketing is expensive and requires a high level of expertise and resources. Individual hotels, attractions and even destinations may not be prominent enough to promote themselves effectively overseas. Most can benefit from the economies of scale of a marketing consortium, particularly if the overseas market is not yet well-established.

Using a consortium approach also benefits the consumer who is offered a more complete 'product' which may be easier to buy than when individual organisations promote their smaller scale products.

Profile raising

Organisations can join together to pool their resources and raise their profile. Unless the products are particularly different or newsworthy, consortia are more capable of stimulating press coverage than small individual organisations. This is particularly true in the accommodation sector where small guesthouses or bed and breakfast operators do not have the resources to use PR effectively. Individual organisations working in isolation can find it difficult to create a strong identity on their own.

Discussion forum

Consortia can provide an opportunity for members to air common problems, compare visitor numbers or occupancy levels and talk about ways of increasing them. Such discussion forums will often go on to undertake joint marketing activities as a result.

When marketing activities grow in this way, there is usually stronger commitment from members than when a central body such as a tourist board suggests them.

Reducing marketing costs

One of the benefits of some consortia is that they can reduce costs. Some consortia come together informally with just one purpose: to share the cost of exhibition stands, particularly at overseas exhibitions.

Strategic planning

Individual organisations can find it difficult to plan far ahead because they are too involved in the day-to-day management of their own operations. It may be difficult for them to target developing markets which have a low awareness of their products.

Consortia can take a longer-term view and work to develop new markets for the common good, rather than for immediate returns. Another benefit of consortia whose main focus is strategic planning is that they offer members access to information such as research data which is otherwise too expensive for individual organisations.

It can sometimes be difficult to get support for this type of consortium, because they require significant resources and are not as action-oriented as some other forms.

Piggy-back promotions

Some of the most powerful, but unfortunately least common, consortia are those which combine organisations from different areas of the tourism industry and organise joint promotions. For example, hotels and attractions can piggy-back on each others' promotions. Hotels need attractions to draw guests to the area, and attractions benefit from the hotel guests.

Developing or improving marketing consortia

Marketing consortia are becoming more popular as organisations realise that they can become more powerful under one umbrella. It is important to realise that most consortia will only have a limited life-span. They are usually set up to deal with a particular issue or type of promotion and at some time the consortia will become redundant or lose momentum. A new consortium may result.

If you are considering setting up a consortium it is essential to be very clear about your objectives. Just as consortia benefit from the combined power of their members, they can also come to resemble unwieldy committees. As everyone knows, any decision made or thing designed by committee can take forever and be unsuccessful. Here are some points you will need to consider.

▓ Consider your objectives carefully and jot them down in writing. This will help to clarify your thoughts and may act as a constitution for the group. It is possible that as the size of the group grows and people introduce their personal agendas, the consortium will change. This may be desirable but it may also be useful to look back at the consortium's original objectives.

▓ It is also useful to consider in advance how big you want the consortium to become, and if you will have specific membership criteria.

▓ Consider how the consortium will be funded and operated. This is critical. If you are going to have a straightforward discussion forum which occasionally undertakes self-financing marketing activities life will be relatively simple. If you want to offer a range of benefits it will be more complex.

▓ You will need to decide whether members will be charged a membership fee, perhaps on a sliding scale depending on the size of their organisation and relative benefits to them. Will the membership fee cover the cost of all activities or will they pay an additional fee for every activity. Bear in mind that it is time consuming to get approval and collect funds for individual activities. Some of the most successful consortia charge quite significant membership fees which cover most activities.

▓ There is a certain amount of administration connected with collecting membership fees. You might decide to charge only for specific activities. However, remember that paying a membership fee is a sign of commitment and members are sometimes more active if they have been charged. You may also need to charge a fee to cover central administration of the consortium.

▓ Consortia with only a handful of members can survive without a paid administrator or marketing co-ordinator. They depend on the goodwill of members and require that as well as doing their existing job, someone will undertake additional activities. This only works when members have spare time and understanding employers. Their loyalty will always be to the organisation which pays their salary so the consortium cannot expect too much from them. For most consortia the only real way forward is to employ at least a part-time administrator or co-ordinator.

▓ Make sure you devise a firm plan of action which is presented to members (preferably just once a year to avoid endless debates) and used as a yardstick to measure the group's progress. Ensure that you have prioritised market segments, agreed a programme of promotional activities and costs. You will generally find it easier if you agree a full programme than ask members to commit to individual activities. Remember to allocate tasks and be specific about who is responsible for implementing the programme.

Pitfalls to avoid

You should beware of several pitfalls into which consortia can fall:

Trying to do everything by committee

Consensus is useful but time-consuming. Successful consortia usually have a strong leader who is committed to moving forward. They should ask for members' approval but not indulge in lengthy consultation debates. There will always be some objections – you will need to let the majority rule, not get side-tracked by the minority.

Inertia

The initial enthusiasm and energy which developed the consortium in the first place will not always be there. If you have set down a firm action plan with deadlines and allocated tasks, members' inertia will be less of a problem.

Insufficient funds

Consortia can help to reduce the costs of promotional activities but they do need sufficient resources to move forward. Beware of charging low subscription rates to recruit members because large memberships are time-consuming and costly to service.

Lack of direction

Your consortium can avoid this problem if you set clear objectives at the outset and have a strong leader. Beware of offering your members too many benefits and services. This can be confusing and counter-productive. Sometimes it is better to agree on one major purpose or activity rather than offering several.

Membership benefits and services

You will not want to overload members with too much information, which they do not have time to read. You will probably be alarmed at the number of members who do not react promptly to mailings, even when they are beneficial to them. Mailings with more than three items are off-putting. If you need to send several forms with details of different options and activities, you can maximise the effect of each if you print each one on different brightly coloured sheets of paper.

You may wish to offer some or all of the following membership benefits:

▓ joint promotional literature;

▓ joint newsletter – for the public or trade;

▓ joint PR campaign;

▓ joint advertising campaign;

▓ joint ticketing schemes such as season tickets to a variety of attractions;

▓ shared stands at exhibitions;

▓ discussion and network meetings;

▓ joint sales missions;

▓ information provision such as market research material or training sessions.

WORKING WITH TOURIST BOARDS

The tourist boards are not exactly promotional tools, but by working with them you will have access to a wider range of promotional opportunities.

National Tourist Boards

Each area of Britain is covered by an area or regional tourist board and also by the Scottish, English, Wales and Northern Ireland Tourist Boards. The remits and responsibilities of these tourist boards vary but their activities generally include:

▓ co-ordination of promotional activities;

▓ strategic guidance and advice to tourism organisations;

▓ monitoring of quality and standards, such as evaluation of accommodation providers;

▓ liaison with local authorities, regional and national government to ensure that tourism is represented in policy decisions; and

▓ improving consumer access to information and ease of purchase by helping to establish effective information and booking channels.

Tourist information centres

The network of tourist information centres are managed and run in a variety of ways, depending on the area of the country and funding structure. They are an important feature of the tourism industry, providing information and help for local residents as well as domestic and overseas visitors. The range of services provided varies but usually includes some or all of the following:

▓ information about places to visit, usually within a 50-mile radius;

▓ information about places to stay and accommodation lists – some tourist information centres offer an accommodation booking service for the local or other areas;

▓ information about local facilities such as restaurants, sporting facilities and general 'what's on' information;

▓ travel information; and

▓ a selection of brochures, maps, guides and tickets, some of which may be for sale.

You can use tourist information centres as a channel of distribution and communication. It is certainly worth taking the time to build positive relationships with tourist information staff because they are in a position to influence the public, and pass on information about what visitors want.

Make sure you keep information centres supplied with the material they need to promote your product, and do not hesitate to ask their advice when developing new products or considering how you will distribute promotional print.

Regional and area tourist boards

You are more likely to work with your regional or area tourist board than directly with the national tourist boards.

Membership fees vary from region to region, usually on a rising scale according to the size of the organisation. As well as giving you access to promotional activities organised by the national tourist boards and the BTA, membership services generally include:

- ▒ marketing advice and expertise;
- ▒ entries in publications, ranging from general destination guides to special interest brochures;
- ▒ the opportunity to take stand space at selected exhibitions or to take part in workshops and seminars;
- ▒ the opportunity to rent mailing lists;
- ▒ sales leads;
- ▒ opportunities to meet other members and share common concerns;
- ▒ access to information and statistics about tourism activity in your area;
- ▒ access to training courses.

Getting the most from your tourist board

Before you commit yourself to joining your tourist board, ask exactly what benefits you will get from membership and make sure you take advantage of them all.

You will probably be asked to fill in a form describing your services, in a set number of words. Make sure you do so, carefully considering the words you use. This short description is likely to be used in several publications going to a wide audience so make sure you stress your unique selling point and key benefits.

The key to benefiting from tourist board membership is involvement: go (or send a representative) to all your tourist board's meetings to which you are invited. You need to make sure you know what is happening in your area, use the opportunity to gather information about local developments and find out about your competitor's activities.

Remember, your tourist board has many members all competing for attention. You must make sure that you are as prominent as possible. The members who shout loudest are most likely to be heard.

Introduce yourself to the staff, particularly those working in any tourist information centres, and invite them to sample your product so they understand what you are offering and can promote it. If they are busy, it might be worthwhile offering to do a short presentation at the tourist information centres premises.

If you do not think you are getting value for money, do not just let your membership lapse. Speak to your tourist board and suggest the kind of services you need. They all need to keep their members to survive so they should be driven by you. As membership organisations, feedback is important to them.

WORKING WITH CONSULTANTS

There are some projects or aspects of promotional activities which you may find difficult to do yourself. Do not worry, there is an army of consultants waiting to help you – for a fee. That is perhaps where the worry starts.

Consultants are sometimes accused of borrowing their client's watch in order to tell them the time. How do you stop them from just being expensive duplicators of previous work? Or from making you dependent on them? Good consultants are like good parents. When you need them they should help you, but at the same time guide you and help you to learn to be independent, so they are no longer needed.

Employing consultants should not necessarily be seen as the expensive option. Indeed, it can be cheaper than retaining full-time staff with specialist knowledge and skills, which you do not always need. A good consultant will provide an objective third party view and should have positive long term effects.

Choosing the cheapest consultant you can find is not always the best option. You generally get what you pay for, although there are limits and there is not necessarily a huge difference in talent between the huge multi-national consultancies and smaller independent ones, although the former will certainly charge you more.

It is worth shopping around to find someone who understands your business, and is enthusiastic about it. You will get more out of a project if you can choose someone with whom you think you will enjoy working.

Getting value for money from consultants

Following these simple guidelines should help you to get value for money.

Set clear objectives: What do you want the consultancy project to achieve?

Few consultants are mind readers. Before you begin interviewing or briefing them, make sure you have clearly defined objectives. Many unsuccessful consultancy relationships or projects are due to inadequate briefing.

Do you want an action plan or a detailed strategy document? Explain your needs fully and do not be shy of revealing any hidden agendas. For example, if you need the results of a project to put before other committees in order to obtain funding, you should say so. Your expectations may be unrealistic in terms of perhaps wanting the consultants to deliver a particularly positive report, when perhaps the situation is not so good.

You should give the consultants the opportunity to evaluate the project and to give you a clear indication of whether or not they can do what you are asking. Describe current practices and recent developments so the potential consultant has a clear understanding of your situation and needs.

Have you found the right consultant?

Make sure the consultant you choose is the right one for your project. Be wary of companies who do not have relevant expertise and subcontract to freelance consultants over whom they have less control (and to whom they pay a far lower fee than you have paid them!).

Ask for examples of past projects and if you can speak to past clients about the consultant's work. Find out if there is any kind of 'after-sales service'. What happens once the project is finished? Will you be able to ask advice about specific aspects at a later date without charge? Good consultants will be interested in making sure you can implement project reports, because their reputation is also based on your success.

Are you committed to the project?

Not only can you learn more by being fully involved, but it is likely to cost less that way. If you are involved you can offer relevant information and contacts, or look at some aspects of research.

Are you prepared to implement the findings of the project?

Before you begin the project, consider how you will implement any findings. Be open-minded: you might disagree with some of the findings or have to make difficult decisions about staffing or expenditure. Consider how you will deal with such issues, before you have to confront them.

Some clients seem to believe that all their problems can be solved by commissioning a consultant's report. This might sometimes be true, but projects will only be successful if you implement recommendations.

What resources can you allocate to the project?

In addition to the budget you will allocate for the consultant's fee you will need to decide what staff resources you can give to the project. How many staff will be involved in any consultative process? How much time can you dedicate to it or would you prefer the consultants to simply 'get on with it'?

Do not just look at the consultant's daily rate. Make sure they state the total number of days they are likely to spend on the project and find out what will happen if time over-runs. Establish what additional charges there are for any expenses so you can establish an overall project fee.

What information already exists?

Do not pay a consultant to gather information which you already have or could easily assemble. Ensure you list and make available any relevant reports or data so the consultant does not waste time (or charge you!) for duplicated work.

What is your time-scale for the project?

Set realistic deadlines and insist on regular update meetings. Do not brief a consultant and expect them to go away for a few weeks and come back with a thick report for you. Much of the value of employing a consultant is in working together to develop suitable proposals.

Suggest project stages so you ensure the consultant works along the lines you envisaged. This will prevent them from mis-understanding your brief and spending time on aspects which you do not wish to cover.

Remember to include time in the project for the consultant to gather and evaluate information, which may come from a variety of sources. This will not affect the number of consultancy days charged but will make a difference to the project time-scale.

What format should the report take?

Make sure that if a report is the outcome of the project, it is practical and easy to implement. Tell the consultant what format you prefer and explain how the report will be used. For example, do you need a detailed financial report for your bank manager or a straightforward action plan for your staff?

Not satisfied with the project?

If you feel the consultant has not addressed the issues outlined in the brief, or delivered a useful report, do not wait for the final invoice before you complain. Discuss your doubts as early as possible so mistakes and misinterpretations can be rectified.

Finding a good consultant

A large proportion of reputable consultants working in the tour-ism industry are members of the Tourism Society Consultants' Group. To help tourism organisations to get the best from con-sultants, they have all signed a declaration of good practice, which is reproduced overleaf.

You can obtain a copy of the *Tourism Society Consultants' Group Directory* free of charge from:

The Tourism Society
26 Chapter Street
London
SW1P 4ND
Telephone: 0171 834 0461
Fax: 0171 932 0238

Declaration of good practice

According to this, consultants should:

▓ maintain high standards of professional endeavour and service, commercial integrity, financial propriety and personal conduct;

▓ accept an engagement only if suitably skilled and experienced to undertake it, and only if it presents no conflict of interest;

▓ agree the terms of the brief and conditions of an engagement with the client, define the services and end products to be provided, identify staff and/or sub-consultants to be employed and clearly specify all financial arrangements;

▓ exercise independence of thought and action in developing recommendations specifically for each client's needs, based on sound research, validated research material, thorough analysis and professional judgement;

▓ ensure that information about their experience and previous commissions is factual and free from statements which are misleading or unfair;

▓ carry out all work diligently and strive to contribute to the reputation and promotion of tourism and leisure consultancy.

4

CASE STUDIES AND EXAMPLES OF GOOD MARKETING

LONDON TOURIST BOARD

Using market research to reposition London and develop a new marketing campaign

The tourism industry is one of the largest in the world and is growing rapidly between 6–8 per cent per year. Britain and London were losing their market share of tourism spend, growing annually at only 2 per cent, and action was needed to correct this trend.

The BTA is responsible for marketing Britain in overseas countries. As the primary brand, London had received much attention, but had not had a unique identity of its own. London had therefore become associated with the more traditional British attributes of culture, arts, pageantry and heritage, and while these remained important, London is also modern, technologically advanced and has excellent nightlife and shopping facilities. It was felt that these aspects were capable of appealing to new and rapidly growing market segments.

The London Tourist Board wanted to substantially increase the revenue received from visitors to London, both for business and leisure. It was therefore necessary to *reposition London as modern, vibrant and the single greatest city in the world*, encouraging existing visitors to reassess their traditional view of the capital and its role as the gateway to Britain, and to stimulate new visitors' interest.

The initial task was to create an umbrella identity for London under which all marketing activity by the public and private sectors could be co-ordinated. This identity or 'brand marque' would serve to bring together the disparate parts of the visitor 'experience' into a focused whole, creating a common theme.

The brand marque would ideally show London as offering diversity in culture, the arts, glamour, entertainment and heritage unmatched by any other single city, in a safe, friendly, economically stable and English-speaking environment.

For the business market it had to be capable of use in supporting London's position as a centre of excellence for communications, finance and support services.

A secondary benefit of the new identity for London was that it would position the capital more positively in the eyes of the UK population and residents of the city.

The development of the new identity for London was a major challenge largely because of the city's diversity and the wide range of market conditions in which it would be applied. The core identity was to remain robust but flexible; capable of being used in both leisure and business situations, in worldwide and domestic markets, in print, advertising, merchandising and sales promotion situations. It had to complement third-party brands including existing tourism initiatives and had to be sensitive to cultures across the world.

In order to develop the new marque and marketing campaign, research was commissioned to explore the current image of London, compared with other key and competing cities such as New York.

Research method and sample

▓ Three focus groups were held in London, Hamburg, New York and Singapore.

▓ Each group had an ABC1 profile, and was of mixed sex and marital status.

- People chosen for the research were those who said they would consider taking a city holiday (and specifically London).

- There were three age bands: 18–24, 25–35, 36–50.

- Qualified, professional researchers were able to guide the discussion, and probe where necessary to develop *qualitative* information.

The focus groups suggested the following factors were important for an 'Ideal City':

- 'something to see, something to buy';

- culture/museums;

- landmarks;

- easy access/good transport;

- range of accommodation;

- good restaurants;

- shopping;

- safety;

- action/nightlife (young).

Comparisons were made with some other major capital cities. Key associations were:

London

- tradition/history;

- historical landmarks (Buckingham Palace, Tower Bridge, the Houses of Parliament and Big Ben);

- royalty;

- cold, damp, rain (especially USA);

- entertainment (musicals/theatre and young music scene);

▨ The Thames;

▨ shopping (especially Singapore);

▨ fleamarkets (especially Germany);

▨ pubs/beer.

Paris

▨ fashion;

▨ romance;

▨ landmarks (Eiffel Tower);

▨ arts/culture;

▨ lifestyle/sidewalk cafes;

▨ good food;

▨ language problem.

New York

▨ urban landmarks (Statue of Liberty, Empire State Building, Wall Street);

▨ skyscrapers;

▨ big, bustling metropolis, traffic and noise – 'a city that never sleeps';

▨ size (especially Germany);

▨ multi-cultural;

▨ nightlife;

▨ crime rate (especially Singapore);

▨ exciting city (especially UK).

Sydney

▨ Opera House (stronger than Harbour Bridge);

▨ koala bears;

▨ beach, barbecue, sport;

▨ no culture.

Hong Kong

▨ crowded, busy;

▨ Chinese food;

▨ hi-tech/electronics (not Singapore);

▨ shopping (Singapore).

The mood of each of these cities was considered to be:

London

▨ traditional, historical ('lots to see');

▨ civilised ('gentleman');

▨ young music scene;

▨ educational (Singapore).

Paris

▨ romantic, elegant, 'soft' *but* people snobbish, arrogant.

New York

▨ High energy, dynamism *but* aggressive.

Sydney

▨ Outdoor, fun, relaxed *but* 'clean, calm and a bit boring'.

Hong Kong

▨ Crowded, busy.

The focus groups were asked how they thought of these key cities. For example, if London was an animal, what animal would it be?

London

- lion (royalty);
- horse (nobility);
- greyhound (hunting);
- bulldog (UK);
- sheep (USA = wet and soggy);
- owl (Singapore = wisdom/education);
- dog (USA = friendly and fun);
- terrier ('small but loud' Singapore).

Paris

- cat (elegant but also distant and sly in USA);
- poodle (stuffy, over-styled);
- peacock (arrogant);
- butterfly/parrot (colour/fashion).

New York

- big cat (fierce, aggressive, powerful).

If each of the cities was a colour, which one would it be?

London

- grey (weather);
- brick colour (buildings);
- purple (nobility/royalty);
- royal blue;
- letter-box red.

Paris

- red (passion);

- ▨ pink (romance);
- ▨ gold/yellow (night lights, Singapore).

New York

- ▨ silver/metallic (blinding);
- ▨ red (vibrant, danger);
- ▨ yellow (cabs).

Who did the group think of as visiting these cities?

London

- ▨ young (music scene) *but* also older;
- ▨ single *and* family;
- ▨ well-educated (Singapore);
- ▨ not adventurous (same language).

Paris

- ▨ honeymooners;
- ▨ single *and* family;
- ▨ young *and* old.

New York

- ▨ businesspeople;
- ▨ young/not family;
- ▨ go-getters;
- ▨ brave (Singapore).

Research summary

The research revealed some important information about London's image:

- ▨ London is most strongly associated with history and tradition.

▨ Although its royal connections are still important, the association is weakening.

▨ Many people associate London with rainy weather but this is not necessarily a barrier because there is enough to see and do.

▨ Britain's reputation for bad food used to be considered a barrier for a trip to London but this is no longer so. There is strong awareness of the many foreign restaurants.

▨ London has a wide range of entertainment for all ages: theatre and musicals, alternative music scene.

▨ London is seen as less aggressive than New York, but not as romantic as Paris – 'Like a wise old man, relaxed, so old and experienced just watching things go by, not vibrant like New York' (comment from the Singapore focus group).

▨ London's image is generally more fragmented than for other cities.

The focus groups in each country were asked to rate the different images of London (see Table).

London image ratings

	UK	Germany	US	Singapore
Friendly	5.2	7.1	7.0	7.7
Modern	5.5	4.5	3.8	5.3
Good nightlife	9.0	7.4	7.1	6.9
Clean	2.4	5.5	6.8	6.3
Good restaurants	7.8	5.1	4.5	6.5
Lively	8.5	7.9	6.6	6.4
Fashionable	7.8	7.2	7.2	7.1
Cosmopolitan	6.2	6.0	3.9	5.3
Expensive	5.1	4.3	5.0	5.4
Good for tourists	7.5	7.9	7.4	7.8
Romantic	6.1	4.5	5.6	6.1
Rich	6.0	5.1	6.0	6.6
Sunny	4.1	3.6	2.7	4.9

The focus groups were shown some initial ideas for logos for London. None of them were considered overwhelmingly appropriate or attractive. The image of London is dominated by tradition and history – a strong reason for rejecting the current logos was the lack of these key elements. It was decided that although the new logo should succeed in communicating a more vibrant and contemporary image for London, traditional elements could not be ignored.

The new logo could not be expected to shoulder the entire repositioning of London – much of which must come from other forms of communication, such as advertising and promotion – 'London is so much to so many people that it would be hard to encapsulate it in a logo, so the simpler the better'.

The results of the research were that the new logo should:

- introduce aspects of contemporary interest without losing focus on the traditional strengths and unique attractions of London (versus other major capitals);

- look 'corporate' and avoid the temptation to be too fashionable (it should be a motif that will last at least a decade without looking dated);

- work in all media (eg on TV, in print, on the Internet) and in both colour and black and white;

- have a broad base appeal (both for business and leisure, both for London and other countries);

- not be too celebratory or festival related, but have a year round relevance;

- capitalise on Britain's brand equity by taking advantage of the national colours.

It was recommended that the design agency should develop alternative designs which concentrate on representing those aspects of London which differentiate it from other capital cities:

- history;

- tradition;

▓ landmarks;

▓ national colours;

▓ British nostalgia/ 'civilised'.

The resulting marque is reproduced below. It can be seen in different ways: sometimes looking modern, vibrant and moving as expressed by the outward-looking dancers, and at other times looking more traditional as expressed by the crown.

© 1996 London Tourist Board Ltd

The new identity was launched nationally by the Secretary of State to the visitor industry and travel trade in 1996. It has already been widely adopted and used by some very varied organisations:

▓ London's only rugby league team, the London Broncos, will be using the marque on their kit, around the perimeter of their ground, on their programme and on all promotional material. All of their games are broadcast worldwide by Sky Television to an audience of around 140 million viewers per match.

▓ The London marque will be prominently displayed on 20 of London Coaches' sightseeing buses.

▓ The Port of London Authority will be flying flags with the London marque at all of their main piers along the River Thames.

- London Transport will be using the marque on all of their overseas leaflets which have a total print run of eight million. The brand marque will also appear on the inside of some of London's buses.

- United Airlines has played the London marque (which has been designed so it can be made to 'move and dance' too) on their video on some domestic flights and run a piece on it in their frequent flyer newsletter which has a circulation of three million in the USA.

- Eighteen giant posters of London incorporating the marque were put up at Victoria Pier at Terminal 4 at London Heathrow airport.

- Channel One TV is using the London marque to brand a new video channel called Inside London.

- The marque was used on 10,000 carrier bags at World Travel Market in 1996.

- The Museum of London flew banners with the London marque on in their new London Now Gallery.

A range of merchandising is being developed including sweatshirts, ties and baseball hats for sale through various outlets.

The brand marque is not just for use as a logo, it also acts as a focus for other marketing activities. In October 1996 the first major advertising campaign incorporating the marque was used by the London Tourist Board and Convention Bureau to promote a more modern and vibrant image of London to overseas visitors. The campaign was run in the USA and France for six months, targeting high-spending visitors via national press and consumer magazines.

In the USA the campaign was designed to challenge the more traditional perceptions of London held by Americans, with a series of striking and powerful images under the banner: London's Wild.

Research had shown that the average American tends to think of London as a bit of a living museum, whereas there are plenty of modern areas offering excellent fashion shops, nightlife and restaurants. The USA market is an important market for London, with Americans spending upwards of £1.2 billion annually in the capital.

The advertising campaign incorporated the new London identity and targeted affluent urban professionals based in New York, Chicago, Boston, Los Angeles, San Francisco and Washington.

At the same time, a campaign was launched in France, aimed at the short-breaks market and targeting three main groups which research had highlighted as having good potential for growth and high propensity to visit London. These groups were single parent families, couples with dual incomes and no kids (sometimes known as 'Dinkies'), and young people aged 18–24.

The advertisements featured the new brand marque and offered a series of persuasive itineraries tailored to each of the three groups, focusing on fun in London, romantic London and trendy London. They appeared in a range of key French national newspapers and magazines, as well as on a special London Tourist Board site on the video-text system, Minitel, which has over 16 million regular users.

The campaign will develop and continue over at least a three-year period, using the results of the research to focus on new markets and to reposition London so it appeals to a wider market.

DISCOVER ISLINGTON

Marketing on a shoestring budget: the power of PR and the importance of niche markets

Islington is a relatively small inner London borough. Although it is just a few tube stops from Oxford Circus, Islington is not on the beaten tourist track. One of its main attractions, Camden Passage Antiques Market attracts considerable visitor numbers but much of it is only open a couple of days a week and is not representative of all that Islington has to offer. Islington lacks prominent attractions with a national reputation, but has great diversity in terms of its small theatres, galleries, restaurants, bars, shops and squares.

Whereas most boroughs or areas are promoted directly by a local authority and/or tourist board, Islington has an unusual arrangement. Discover Islington is an arm's length agency and was set up as a company limited by guarantee. It is funded by the local authority and various other sources including the Training and Enterprise Council, Single Regeneration Budget work, private sector sponsorship and revenue generating activity.

Its aims are 'to improve perceptions of the area, enhance local facilities and infrastructure and help create job opportunities though increased revenue from visitors, balancing the benefit to visitors with the benefit to those living and working in the area'. It does all this, as well as operating a visitor information centre, on a fraction of the budget which many organisations spend on a single project.

In the past, Islington Council had invested considerable sums of money in exhibition attendance, advertising and publication of a plethora of leaflets. These included titles as diverse as: *The Clock Tower and Environs*, *John Perry Wallpapers*, *Banking in Islington*, and my personal favourite, *A Veritable Land of Cows – the Agriculture of Islington*. Unfortunately there was no real consideration of potential target markets and little monitoring to judge the tangible (or otherwise!) results of such promotions.

Under the leadership of Helen Carpenter, Discover Islington (created in 1991 with the backing of the English Tourist Board) recognised the importance of identifying clear target markets. It was clear that Islington did not offer 'something for everyone' and did not have extensive resources, in terms of budgets or staff. A tourism strategy was produced in 1992, with an updated marketing plan in 1994.

As well as promoting the area, Discover Islington also runs the visitor information centre. Information is provided free of charge, but efforts are also made to generate income to offset the centre's costs, while endeavouring to offer a wide range of services. For example, a small fee is made for accommodation. A wide range of publications and gifts are for sale within the information centre.

A considerable proportion of Islington's staying visitors come to visit their friends and relatives. Discover Islington therefore needs to make local people aware of their services. This will raise revenue in the visitor information centre and encourage visitors to spend more time in Islington rather than visiting other areas of London.

It was recognised that the types of London visitors who are most likely to enjoy Islington are:

▓   repeat visitors, therefore less likely to want to visit 'must see' attractions such as the Tower; and/or

▓   people who do not consider themselves 'tourists'. This could be because they are simply visiting friends and relatives or because they have a non-tourist approach. For example, younger visitors often want to experience London's nightlife rather than go to museums.

For anyone looking for the 'real London', Islington represents the ideal destination, with a diverse range of evening activities.

A key priority was the need to raise awareness of Islington's facilities. Local residents needed to know more about the facilities on their doorstep and to learn about the services of the visitor information centre.

Discover Islington also knew that there would be strong interest from young Europeans if only they had more information about Islington. Simply approaching the BTA overseas offices was not enough. The BTA are responsible for the promotion of a myriad of products, and simply do not have the time or resources to promote smaller areas such as Islington. They have to give priority to the better known 'icons'.

Target markets

Islington had to target its markets at a variety of levels:

People living and working in Islington

Islington's residents are an important market. They can be encouraged to spend more of their leisure time in Islington if they know more about what is on offer. Those living nearby can be enticed into the Visitor Information Centre to buy their stamps, phonecards and small gifts, as well as acting as valuable word of mouth 'influencers' to visitors to Islington.

Existing visitors, eg antique hunters

It is always easier to attract more visitors who are similar to existing ones, than to develop completely new markets. The affluent visitors who enjoy Camden Passage Antiques Market remain important.

Developing markets: independent young Europeans

Young Europeans, and particularly Germans and Dutch were found to be one of the principle markets for the 'younger' Islington product combination of nightlife and trendy shops. These independent travellers are looking for experiences which give them a different insight into London 'life'.

It was important to develop a profile of these different markets and to understand their needs. With a limited budget, Discover Islington realised that PR activities would be one of the most cost-effective promotional tools they could use.

Reaching the target markets

Just as the target markets vary, so do the channels by which they can be reached:

People living and working in Islington

Helen Carpenter has written articles about various aspects of Islington as well as being the subject of several features in the local press. The Discover Islington Visitor Information Centre is gradually raising awareness of its facilities within the local area, and visitor numbers are increasing and are currently around 20,000 per annum. Turnover and profit are also increasing.

Another positive development is the creation of Discover Islington Network, a relatively informal membership consortium of some 80 or 90 local businesses whose members meet on a regular basis. Each meeting is held in a different location and there is a strong element of socialising so that members become more aware of Islington's rich diversity.

Existing visitors, eg antique hunters

The affluent antique hunters can be reached through in-flight magazines and particularly through magazines distributed through hotels in central London, such as the *Dorchester* magazine, which has given Islington good coverage.

Developing markets: independent young Europeans

Independent travellers such as young Germans rely heavily on guidebooks for their information, so a list of guidebook editors has been developed. Efforts are being made to ensure that guidebook entries about Islington are accurate and truly representative.

At the same time, press releases and information have been sent to a wide variety of media contacts. Discover Islington has been particularly successful in securing large-scale coverage in publications such as the German regional press as well as being the subject for a German travel programme.

This effort is now beginning to pay off. The sound of German and Dutch voices in Islington is becoming more and more commonplace. Discover Islington now receives a steady flow of telephone calls and faxes from Germany. Perhaps the strongest indication of the increased demand from the German public was a request from the BTA office in Frankfurt for more information about Islington.

It is more usual, and often more productive for smaller areas to join together to promote themselves, and to do so as part of broader promotions under an area or national tourist board. In Islington's case this was more difficult because of the nature of the product, which is far from 'mainstream'. However, Islington has demonstrated the power of PR, and is gradually positioning itself as an area of London which every young European will want to visit.

HISTORIC ROYAL PALACES

Understanding and supporting the travel trade to increase visitor numbers

Historic Royal Palaces was established as an Executive Agency in 1989, and is responsible for the running of five Historic Royal Palaces:

▨　The Tower of London;

▨　Hampton Court Palace;

▨　Kensington Palace;

▨　the Banqueting House; and

▨　Kew Palace with Queen Charlotte's Cottage within the grounds of the Royal Botanic Gardens at Kew.

The Historic Royal Palaces Agency's remit is to preserve the Palaces for future generations to enjoy. Generating income by attracting optimum visitor numbers forms part of this task.

Historic Royal Palaces wish to attract visitors to each of the palaces, which is obviously easier in the case of the Tower of London than Kew Palace. Until 1992 the Agency did not specifically target the travel trade but there was a growing awareness that its multiple purchasing power could be harnessed to increase visitor numbers dramatically.

Research among selected members of the travel trade indicated that they regarded the Tower of London, and to a certain extent Hampton Court Palace, as a 'must-see' attraction. However, the Historic Royal Palaces Agency had a much lower profile and the travel trade were unable to identify all of the Palaces in its care. The Agency was also seen as a rather faceless organisation which did not always communicate effectively with the trade.

In 1992 the Palaces Agency realised that they needed to adopt a more co-ordinated and proactive strategy to attract group bookings. An Agency Voucher Scheme existed but was not properly promoted and was regarded as 'travel trade un-friendly'. It was believed that much more business could be obtained from the travel trade once a proper strategy was in place to attract group bookings.

Several segments of the travel trade were identified as having good potential to deliver significant visitor numbers:

▓ incoming tour operators;

▓ London sightseeing tour companies;

▓ UK and overseas coach operators with their own programmes;

▓ group tour organisers from the voluntary sector;

▓ incentive and conference organisers.

The objectives of the travel trade strategy were to:

▓ present a more positive image of the Historic Royal Palaces Agency as a whole;

▓ increase visitor numbers to all the palaces;

▓ enhance awareness of, and visits to the smaller, lesser-known palaces.

The palaces needed to change their approach towards the travel trade and to show that their bookings were valued. The travel trade strategy was developed to indicate that the Historic Royal Palaces Agency was actively interested in business from the travel trade and that it now had a much more friendly and flexible approach.

The palaces needed to show that they understood the key needs of the travel trade. For example:

▓ the need for information about price changes, special events, etc at least six months in advance;

▓ the need for information about relevant facilities such as coach parking, group discounts and reasons why the palaces are worth visiting; and

▨ the need to make it easier for operators to make bookings by offering named travel trade contacts for each Palace.

The strategy included a number of key recommendations, all of which Historic Royal Palaces Agency acted on:

Demonstrate commitment to the travel trade and make it easier to book by offering a central contact point

A dedicated travel trade sales office was opened, based at Hampton Court Palace. A sales manager with first-hand experience of the travel trade was recruited, together with administrative support staff. The sales manager spends most of her time dealing directly with the travel trade, as well as developing new products and packages. Administrative support staff based in the office are also proactive and ensure that the work of the sales manager is followed through. Travel trade contacts were also established for each of the individual palaces.

Develop suitable information for the travel trade

A travel trade manual was developed which includes full details about coach parking; descriptions of the palaces; opening times and recommended duration of visits; group admissions procedure; location; admissions charges and group reductions; special facilities and forthcoming events. A quarterly newsletter also updates operators about changes, new facilities and packages.

Offer easy payment facilities

Most tour operators use a voucher system. The tour leader usually presents a voucher on arrival at an attraction, and they are then invoiced after the visit, removing the need for cash payments. The Palaces Agency Voucher System was revamped, making it easier to join the scheme and more attractive to tour operators.

Establish a proactive sales programme

The travel trade sales office is now responsible for a full programme of sales visits to tour operators and group organisers. It also attends various exhibitions and workshops in the UK and overseas. Another aspect of the sales programme is the development of packages which persuade the trade to offer visits to some of the lesser known palaces, such a joint ticket for Hampton Court Palace and nearby Kew Palace.

Since the introduction of the travel trade marketing strategy, the sales manager has taken responsibility for developing other initiatives and joint promotions with various operators and attractions. The travel trade now view the Historic Royal Palace Agency more positively and recognise that the sales office is there to help them exploit the profit opportunities offered by the Palaces. Bookings through the travel trade have increased dramatically and this trend looks set to continue.

PITSHANGER MANOR

Understanding the needs of market segments and developing products to attract them

Pitshanger Manor Museum was originally architect Sir John Soane's country villa, dating back to the early nineteenth century. The Regency villa is set in the attractive surroundings of Walpole Park in the centre of Ealing in West London. Sir John Soane rebuilt most of the house using his rather individual ideas in design and decoration to provide a place to entertain friends and exhibit his collections.

The Manor is now being restored and refurbished in an appropriate style and has become an established arts venue, hosting a range of events including jazz, classical music, children's events and numerous workshops and short courses. Pitshanger Manor is once again being used for similar purposes to when it was first bought by Sir John Soane.

From the outside Pitshanger Manor presents an imposing facade, which some people may even find off-putting. Inside there is a limited amount of furniture and a collection of Martinware pottery. People with a strong interest in Soane's work will find the building of great interest but most visitors would be forgiven for seeing it as just another historic house. Next door to the Manor is a gallery, set in a 1930s library building which was recently opened as West London's largest visual arts space.

Pitshanger Manor Museum and Gallery is owned and run by the London Borough of Ealing. As a local authority venue it is important to make the building available to all local residents. Whereas this type of building would normally attract a 'white, middle-class, middle-aged' profile, arts officer Neena Sohal needed to ensure that the building was not only accessible to all, but also attractive to all sectors of the population, including the strong Asian community.

The first step for Neena Sohal was to research each of the sectors of the community and ensure that their needs were understood. It was unlikely that the Asian community would initially want to visit a house which did not seem to have any relevance to them, unless they were given a reason to do so.

A programme of events was planned which offered a range of activities likely to be of interest to different sets of people. One part of this was a performance by a Punjabi singer, who was a 'living legend' among the Asian community.

The local Asian community was unaware of Pitshanger Manor and what it had to offer. The singer's agreement to perform at Pitshanger Manor offered an ideal opportunity to build a new audience, using the performance to make them aware of the venue. However, it was important to make a really positive and strong impact so there would be plenty of word-of-mouth publicity for future events, and to encourage people to return at other times.

Neena recognised that Pitshanger Manor needs to be adapted for different types of events. She has a strong understanding of the Asian community and their needs, which are not necessarily the same as other groups so she set about creating the right atmosphere for the concert.

A small stage was built and colourful textiles were used as a backdrop. Distinctive and traditional Punjab colour combinations of orange, brown and blue were used for the backdrop, and these colours were also used on the posters advertising the event. Orange flowers were added, together with joss sticks scattered around the room to give it an authentic Punjab feel.

The performance was a sell-out and helped to build visitor numbers. Similar events were staged. Each time they were preceded by a short talk by Neena Sohal, explaining some of the history of the building. This has since led to numerous visits by Asian community groups who have come specifically to tour the building.

The events programme is wide-ranging and includes more traditional events such as string quartets which require a more formal setting. Contemporary theatre is performed in the round and other events cater for different sectors of the local population. Children are given the opportunity to participate in a wide variety of workshops and events designed specially for them.

For each event consideration is given to the type of people they will attract, and how they can be made most comfortable within the villa surroundings. In this way the building has been transformed from an intimidating setting into a more intimate one with a warm and lively atmosphere – just as it would have been when Sir John Soane used it.

More recently, the gallery was re-opened, extending the scope for exhibitions and visual art demonstrations. One of the first events was an exhibition of South African art, which was also used as part of the gallery's launch. South African food was served outside and dancers performed traditional dances on the lawn, juxtaposed with the facade of the Regency villa. The noise from the dancers and small band attracted passing shoppers' attention and drew them into the free exhibition, which in turn directed visitors to explore the rest of the house.

The events programme was begun in 1993 and visitor numbers have more than trebled in the three years since then, demonstrating the value of packaging products to appeal to particular markets.

MACE COURT HOTEL, LONDON

Developing promotional material to appeal to target markets and selling benefits, not features

Within the area of Paddington in London there are countless hotels offering budget accommodation, all competing with each other. The majority of hotels are relatively small, privately owned and correspond to the two-star category. Their facilities are similar, their location is similar and they are all competing for a similar market.

It is difficult for many of these hotels to find a competitive advantage and to stand out from the rest. Hotels in this area have a reputation for budget prices, often with budget service. Service and standards in this type of hotel are improving but they still have to deal with their former reputation as 'bed factories', working on tight margins. Budget hotels have a reputation for often being unfriendly, sometimes dirty and rarely offering any added value.

Most hotels in this category have a very limited marketing budget and only the simplest brochure or flyer with which to promote the hotel. The Mace Court Hotel's brochure stands way above the competition. The owner recognises the importance of some investment in marketing and it has paid off for him.

A professional designer was engaged, as well as a photographer who has made sure the small but value-for-money bedrooms are presented in a good light. Using an A4 format, which folds to one third A4 for easy display in brochure racks, the Mace Court Hotel brochure was not expensive to produce but careful thought went into its design and the words it uses.

Instead of listing facilities as many hotels do, the brochure addresses readers directly and tells them how they will benefit from staying in the Mace Court. It stresses its value for money and goes on to say that means the reader will be able to enjoy their stay in London more, which is easy because the hotel is so centrally located. A simple map shows exactly where the hotel is and how many minutes it takes to reach other key points such as Oxford Circus and some famous museums.

The brochure mentions some of the famous people who lived in or near Paddington, bringing the place alive. It describes some of the most interesting places to visit in Central London, recognising that most of its guests will be first-time visitors who will spend more time out of the hotel than in it.

The brochure uses plenty of pictures, maps and illustrations to make its point instead of wordy copy. It stresses the friendly service offered by all members of staff and uses a bright, but warm style to express cleanliness.

The owner of the Mace Court Hotel pays for extensive distribution of his brochures, and works closely with the Tourist Board. Whenever possible tourist information staff are invited to see the hotel so they can recommend it to others. The owner also personally visits tour operators to sign contracts with them and develop a good relationship.

The investment in marketing has paid off, with higher than average occupancy levels and slightly higher room rates. The Mace Court Hotel does not offer extraordinary facilities, although it is clean, friendly and value for money. But the hotel stands well above other hotels of a similar standard in the same area by telling potential guests what they want to hear – that they will have an enjoyable visit to London, and how easy it is to enjoy.

The name of this hotel has been changed to preserve commercial confidentiality.

DORMOUSE HOTEL, LINCOLNSHIRE

Developing a niche market to compete and develop a profitable business

The Dormouse Hotel in Lincolnshire is a two-star hotel. Its name attracts attention but it offers very similar facilities to other hotels in the area. The Dormouse Hotel used to promote itself heavily to business travellers such as sales representatives but this market has been adversely affected by the recession and heavier competition from new hotels such as Travelodges.

The Dormouse Hotel is run by a single parent, Mrs Banter who relies on the hotel for her livelihood but who would also like to devote more time to her son. They live on the premises so her young son, Michael is often to be seen. Business travellers do not always welcome the sight of a boisterous young child in the hotel lounge.

Some of the similar hotels in the area have gone out of business. Others are investing in new facilities and upgrading but competition is still tough. The Dormouse Hotel's strong point is its beautiful big garden. From time to time children played in it and older people enjoyed sitting there but it was underused.

It was obvious that Mrs Banter's share of the budget business travel market was declining and she needed to develop new markets. She turned to a market which she knows and understands well – single parents and families. There are few hotels which truly cater for this market, and the Dormouse Hotel was an ideal destination. The large garden is an excellent safe place for children to play. Mrs Banter has always offered more facilities for people with children, lending them buggies and toys and providing activity packs based on local places of interest which she developed for her own son.

With a little additional effort, Mrs Banter was able to develop activity packages suitable for different age groups and to provide relaxing value-for-money holidays for children and their parents. This was an ideal solution and a growth market, and the guests did not mind if Michael wanted to join in the fun.

A logo was developed for the hotel which appealed to children and this was used both within the hotel and for new promotions. In Winter the dormouse promoted cosy 'winter warmers' with lots of indoor activities and in summer it came alive to offer outdoor activity breaks, with treasure hunts in the garden.

The breaks are now being offered to a secondary market – older people who either bring their grandchildren with them or who enjoy the sound of children playing around them as they enjoy a game of bridge or canasta.

The Dormouse Hotel has successfully promoted the breaks using press releases to family and women's magazines who often pick up on this unusual hotel. Word-of-mouth publicity has also been invaluable, which Mrs Banter has harnessed by offering vouchers for people who introduce new guests to the hotel. Mailings to parents organisations have also helped to develop interest in the hotel, which is now trading successfully again, capitalising on a growth market and precise market segment which the owner clearly understands.

The name of this hotel has been changed to preserve commercial confidentiality.

WILTSHIRE

Using the findings of a SWOT analysis to develop new markets and promotional activities

Most destinations aim to attract more visitors, and to gain economic benefit from them. Wiltshire already receives high numbers of visitors but is now looking at ways of increasing their economic impact.

Substantial numbers of people come to Wiltshire each year to visit famous sites such as Stonehenge and Avebury but then drive on out of the county to places like Bath. Little economic benefit is derived from such visitors and there is a danger that these sites will become too overcrowded, with the destruction of the very things that people come to experience. Others simply drive through Wiltshire on the way to other areas of the West Country.

Wiltshire County Council and its partners in the district councils clearly needed to look at ways of increasing the positive benefit of tourism in the area.

A SWOT analysis was conducted which included some of the following findings:

Strengths

- excellent location – close to London, Midlands, Bristol, Bath and South Coast ports;

- good range of outdoor activities such as horseriding, cycling and ballooning;

- superb countryside, of a predominantly rural nature;

- attractive towns and villages with many historic houses and gardens;

- low seasonality for accommodation;

- good reputation for country house hotels;

- tourist attractions of national and international renown;

▓ famous and unique sites such as Stonehenge and Avebury;

▓ newly-opened canal networks running across the heart of the county;

▓ few negative image factors;

▓ good range of bed and breakfast and farmhouse accommodation;

▓ good network of tourist information centres.

Weaknesses

▓ location regarded as a place *en route* to somewhere else, mainly the West Country;

▓ lack of visitor knowledge as to where attractions are located;

▓ no coastline environment, therefore does not attract as many families as other West Country destinations;

▓ environmental and visitor management problems associated with some attractions such as Avebury means that these cannot be overtly promoted;

▓ the area has a very low profile and is not viewed as a tourist destination in its own right;

▓ farm tourism is as yet a relatively undeveloped segment;

▓ limited variety of shopping and night life;

▓ county has only recently appointed a tourism officer;

▓ duplication of effort and competition between district council tourism officers.

Opportunities

▓ opening of channel tunnel will improve accessibility;

▓ countryside has many little-known and underused resources and rural tourism is not dictated by as many peaks and troughs as coastal tourism;

▓ canal network has potential for greater use;

▓ increased general demand for activity holidays and short breaks;

▓ farm tourism a growth area;

▓ better co-ordination and co-operation between Wiltshire County Council, District Councils and the Private Sector imminent.

Threats

▓ vulnerable environment;

▓ canal network vulnerable to overuse;

▓ lack of co-ordination of image and local residents wary of tourism;

▓ increased competition from other areas in the UK;

▓ decreased demand for some types of domestic holidays.

Visitor research was limited but it appeared that the following were the main markets:

▓ active senior citizens;

▓ dinkies – couples aged 25–40 without children;

▓ tour groups – but only visiting key sites such as Stonehenge, then moving on to other destinations, often outside Wiltshire;

▓ small but healthy level of business and conference travel, particularly focused round the Swindon area and some of the country house hotels.

The majority of visitors were from the UK, within 2.5 hours' driving distance of Wiltshire, especially from the Midlands and London area. Overseas visitors come from the Netherlands, Germany, France and the USA. The main reasons cited for visiting Wiltshire were:

▓ rural attractions, open spaces and Areas of Outstanding Natural Beauty;

▦ outdoor activities such as cycling and horse-riding;

▦ heritage and history, including the Kennet and Avon Canal.

An audit of previous marketing activities by the County and District Councils highlighted the following key points:

▦ Wiltshire lacked a strong identity and needed to raise aware-ness of its location and assets in order to generate more visitors.

▦ There was a plethora of print material which gave out con-flicting messages and duplicated effort.

▦ Tourism promotion was being undertaken at a variety of levels so there were some areas of overlap.

▦ Distribution channels for many of the Wiltshire products were not clear – it was not 'easy to buy' some products such as activity holidays even though the product was basically good and demand strong. There was inadequate product packag-ing to direct visitors and encourage them to come and to stay in Wiltshire.

Based on this information, workshops were held to try to deter-mine 'What is Wiltshire?' It was agreed that Wiltshire's key selling points are:

▦ its location – less than two hours from London and close to many other interesting places such as Bath;

▦ its unique heritage attractions such as Stonehenge and Ave-bury, which can not be replicated elsewhere;

▦ its ancient woodlands, unspoilt countryside and Areas of Outstanding Natural Beauty and good provision of outdoor activities;

▦ value-for-money accommodation in B&Bs, farms and coun-try house hotels.

It was apparent that Wiltshire needed to promote itself to people who are looking for active short breaks in the countryside, or to enjoy heritage attractions.

A positioning statement was developed, which describes the most important and attractive aspects of Wiltshire:

> rural adventures, outstanding natural beauty and 2000 years of history, just two hours from London

It was important to build on current markets, and to develop others based on some important market trends such as the increased demand for activity holidays and for short breaks.

Geographic markets were selected according to their growth rates and propensity to enjoy countryside holidays. For example, Germany is showing good growth rates, and generates high visitor spend. There is a strong trend to look for 'green' destinations for holidays, offering the opportunity to enjoy the countryside and outdoor pursuits, and to travel off the beaten track.

Within each geographic market, different segments were also specified. For example:

UK

▦ active couples and individuals ABC1 aged 25+, interested in outdoor pursuits and regular short-break takers;

▦ ABC1 older couples, whose families have left home, or who are enjoying an active retirement, predominantly interested in the outdoors or heritage attractions;

▦ travel trade – tour operators specialising in small groups and heritage holidays.

Germany

▦ Repeat visitors (to England) aged 30+, living in the old federal states, with a minimum net monthly household income of DM 4000.

▦ Repeat visitors (to England) aged 45+, well-educated professionals living in the old federal states, with a minimum net monthly household income of DM 5000.

▦ Travel trade – specialist study tour operators such as Studiosus in Munich.The full list of segments was long. Not all of them would be targeted at the same time with the same activities.

A marketing action plan was developed to build on these key recommendations:

▦ Establish an image and identity for Wiltshire, which is communicated through all promotional activities, and particularly on all print material whether it is produced by each of the District Councils or the County Council.

▦ Develop a consortium approach to marketing, which involves the districts, public and private sector (accommodation, attractions, retail, etc).

▦ Improve channels of distribution to make the Wiltshire 'countryside product' easier to buy.

▦ Produce print material which clearly meets the differing needs for pre- and post-arrival information.

▦ Develop methods of 'cross-fertilising' existing visitors to Wiltshire (such as those coming to Stonehenge or the new Factory Shopping Outlet) and increasing their stay and spend in the area.

▦ Develop a co-ordinated public relations campaign to raise the profile of Wiltshire and maintain interest within key markets.

▦ Improve the cost-effectiveness of advertising through careful targeting, media buying and design;

▦ Improve communication between organisations and people working in the tourism industry in Wiltshire, in both the public and private sector.

▦ Set objectives to make exhibition attendance more effective.

▨ Develop direct links with tour operators and encourage them to feature Wiltshire in their brochures and itineraries.

▨ Offer marketing support and training to all tourism suppliers in Wiltshire in order to help them improve their own promotional methods.

▨ Develop better market intelligence and research information about current visitors to Wiltshire, including their profile, motivations and needs, and to establish monitoring mechanisms for all promotions.

Most of these activities are still in their infancy so it will take time before they bear fruit, but there is strong evidence of commitment to the action plan and a positive attitude to make it work with the district authorities now working more closely together to promote Wiltshire as a whole. By working through the marketing strategy together and developing more focused activities, everyone involved in tourism marketing in Wiltshire has been able to make better use of their resources, and become more effective.

INDEX